SOUTH WE

Capital Transport

CONTENTS

ISBN 185414 153 8

Published by Capital Transport Publishing
38 Long Elmes, Harrow Weald, Middlesex

Printed by The KPC Group, Ashford, Kent

© Capital Transport Publishing 1993

The front cover photo is by Barry Spencer
The back cover photos are by Ivor Norman, Keith Grimes and Richard Eversden
The frontispiece is by Ken Jubb

Acknowledgements
We are grateful to David Donati, Keith Grimes, Mark Jameson, Graham Jones,
Colin Lloyd, Allan Macfarlane, Colin Martin, Geoff Mills, the PSV Circle and the operating
companies for their assistance in the compilation of this book.

Contents correct to December 1992
Series Editor: Bill Potter

BADGERLINE

Badgerline Ltd, Oldmixon Crescent, Weston-super-Mare, Avon, BS24 9AX

Badgerline Ltd was formed on 28th November 1985 to take over four of Bristol Omnibus Company's depots and operations and has since grown into one of the big three groups of British bus providers. The original operation was based at Weston and was based on the services which had previously been operated under the 'Bristol Country' fleetname: Bristol (Marlborough Street); Weston-super-Mare (Beach Bus Station); Bath (London Road) and Wells (Priory Road). Badgerline commenced operations on 1st January 1986.

The new company was sold by the NBC to its own management team (plus 100 employees) on 23rd September 1986. A Holding company, Badgerline Holdings Ltd, was formed of which Badgerline Ltd is a subsidiary.

The operational area is bounded by the Bristol Channel in the west, Berkeley and Tetbury in the north, Devizes and Warminster in the east and Frome, Street and Bridgwater in the south. Competitive services were started at Poole, Salisbury and Portsmouth, but these have now either ceased or have been sold leaving just the original four depots still in use. The depot at Weston has since moved to Oldmixon Crescent and the bus station site has been redeveloped.

Original fleet livery consisted of yellow with a broad diagonal stripe in emerald green plus a black skirt; this is being changed to all-over emerald green with large badger motifs. Coaches are in a livery of white, yellow and green while minibuses use the Minilink name and the open top fleet are cream, lime green and brunswick green at Bath, or yellow and green at Weston. Many vehicles also carry the name of their home depot over each front wheel arch in white.

When Thamesway converted its Southend-on-Sea area services to minibus operation in January 1991, several of their Bristol VRs were offered to other Badgerline Group members. Badgerline itself took seven, with a further nine coming in 1992 following the ending of Thamesway's London contracts. No.5551 is seen amid a selection of buses in Badgerline's cheerful yellow and bright green, as it leaves Bath bus station on the 'back route' to Bristol. Allan Macfarlane

In January 1992, Roe-bodied Leyland Olympian 8614 was repainted for assessment in a revised layout of the yellow and green colours, with new-style fleetnames and, most controversially, a huge grinning badger on the sides. The effect is shown in this photograph, which also depicts the luminous-yellow destination blinds now being installed in many of Badgerline's buses. Bristol Vintage Bus Group

Alexander-bodied Volvo Citybus 5709 was the second double-decker to receive the new layout of colours with the large badger emblem. It is expected that this style will be adopted for the more modern types as they are repainted. This batch of a dozen Volvos has always been allocated to Weston-super-Mare. Lee Turton

The five MCW Metrobuses have spent a lifetime based at Bath. Four of them have now received lettering for Bath Park & Ride duties. Occasionally one will appear in normal service as depicted by 6004 heading home from Bristol. G.R. Mills

Impressive vehicles are the two East Lancs-bodied long-wheelbase Leyland Olympians, fitted with 78 coach seats. They were new to Rhymney Valley's Inter Valley Link duties, but now offer a quality ride to Bristol-area travellers. No.5000 is seen at Bath bus station. Martin Curtis

Now in its 30th year is Weston open-topper 8604. It is a Weymann-bodied Leyland Atlantean that was acquired from Maidstone & District in 1980. Weston's open-toppers now carry standard Badgerline colours, but without the white strip above the windows and still featuring the special badger carrying a bucket and spade. G.R. Mills

Bristol-based Leyland Tiger/Duple Laser 2 coaches 2222/3 were the first vehicles to appear with the new lettering for the fleetname and the great grinning badger on the sides, in October 1991. The paint scheme on these is all-over green, which is surprisingly effective. No.2222 is passing through Bath on a limited-stop service. Martin Curtis

All Mark I Leyland Nationals are currently based at Bath. At work on a city service is 3031. Richard Eversden

Some of the Leyland National 2s were re-equipped with coach seats a few years ago and now carry the coach version of the Badgerline livery. This is exemplified by 3517. Allan Macfarlane

The single-deck version of the new livery style is shown here on 101, a Volvo B10M with Alexander P-type bodywork. In prototype form, the front dome was painted green, but reversion to yellow is an improvement. These B10Ms are housed at Weston-super-Mare depot, though their duties include a couple of turns on contracted Bristol city routes 527/528. Lee Turton

Just seven Leyland Lynxes are operated by Badgerline. New in 1990, they are allocated to Wells. No.3612 is seen in Glastonbury on the long 376 Bristol to Yeovil route. Neil Jennings

The Bristol RE is still giving valuable service to Badgerline, even if only to the tune of eight examples now. Twenty-year-old 1257 caused surprise in June 1991 when it appeared specially repainted in an approximation of its original Tilling-green and cream livery, with the Bristol scroll fleetname. (When new, incidentally, it was a dual-doorway Bristol city bus). All REs are stationed at Wells, which is where we see 1257 here. G.R. Mills

Wells attracts sightseers because of its fine Cathedral . . . and bus enthusiasts because of its fine stock of Bristol REs! The newest now left running is 1332, captured here setting off on a regular trip for the REs, to Weston-super-Mare. G.R. Mills

Whereas the first, hefty intake of minibuses consisted of 16-seat Ford Transits, subsequent additions have contained extra seats and luggage space. The Robin Hood-bodied Iveco 49-10, with 19 seats, was chosen in 1986/87 and is represented here by 4904/5. The location is on the northern fringe of Badgerline's territory, at Dursley. Colin Martin

Associated operator Western National only received one batch of Ford Transits and in 1987, when only a year old, they were transferred to Badgerline. Unlike the native stock, these are on the new style Transit; their bodies were finished by Dormobile, with rather smaller windows than on their earlier versions. No.4597 rests at Bath bus station. G.R. Mills

Currently, Badgerline has just 20 midibuses. These are Optare StarRiders, based on Mercedes-Benz 811D chassis. They are 31-seaters, except for four, which contain 27 coach seats. Seen in Weston is 3802, waiting time on the Avon County supported version of the 126 service, numbered 826. Bristol Vintage Bus Group

Recently coming into service are the first 17 of a new generation of minibuses for Badgerline, 23-seat Mercedes-Benz 709Ds, with Plaxton Beaver bodywork. They carry the all-over green livery previously confined to two coaches, whereas their numbering is an extension of the series for midibuses. No.3852 and all its present consorts work at Weston-super-Mare. BVBG

The Bath open-top city tour is very popular and requires a sizeable fleet to cater for the tourists. A Bristol VR brought in from Western National, in exchange for a fixed-top VR, is 8606, named Minerva. The tour is run in conjunction with the well-known Guide Friday organisation and the lettering on the buses is to the Guide Friday house style. Keith Wood

Popular with tourists and bus enthusiasts alike is 8583, the 1941 Bristol K5G. It was originally a Bristol city bus, but was sold to Brighton Hove & District in 1955, where it was rebuilt to the style now familiar. After further service at Port Talbot, it returned to Bristol ownership in 1969. It was fully renovated for Bath Tour work in 1990 and is seen on one of its regular Saturday outings. Keith Wood

CHELTENHAM & GLOUCESTER

Cheltenham & Gloucester Omnibus Company Ltd, Bath Street, Cheltenham, GL50 1YE
Swindon & District Bus Company Ltd, Bath Street, Cheltenham, GL50 1YE

The company was formed in September 1983 to take over the northern area of Bristol Omnibus services together with depots at Stroud (London Road), Gloucester (London Road), Cheltenham (St Marks) and Swindon (Eastcott Road). The operational area extends to Tewkesbury in the north, Faringdon and Oxford in the east, Marlborough, Wotton-under-Edge and Dursley in the south and the Bristol Channel in the west.

Each of the depots has its own livery and fleetname, a practice started in the initial days of the company, then still owned by the National Bus Company.

On purchase of the company from National Bus Company in 1986 a holding company, Western Travel Ltd, was formed. In December 1991 the Swindon & District fleet was split off as a separate unit with some thirty-seven vehicles. This was initially known as Fouray 319 Ltd, but was later renamed 'Swindon & District Bus Company Ltd', though it continues as part of Western Travel.

Current livery schemes are: Cheltenham, red with cream stripe; Gloucester, blue with yellow stripe; Stroud, green with yellow stripe and Swindon, red with cream stripe. Minibuses are silver with red and blue stripes and coaches are in various colours depending on their contracts.

Leyland's integral Titan design of the late 1970s became a rare bird outside London and, to an extent, Reading. So Swindon is perhaps privileged to host five Titans. They were not new here, but to Greater Manchester Transport and even after that worked for South Midland. No.109 retains its Manchester destination screens. Compare the Park Royal bodywork with the Roe and ECW Olympians elsewhere in this book. G.R. Mills

Inherited from Bristol Omnibus Company at Cheltenham & Gloucester's formation were the Leyland Olympians with Roe bodywork. Their electronic destination screens were fairly soon replaced by conventional blinds, as exemplified by 9521. This Cheltenham District bus is seen setting off for home from Gloucester. Martin Curtis

Five new Olympians arrived at Swindon in 1990. These differed from those already in stock in several ways, but most notably in being long-wheelbase models with Alexander R-type bodywork seating 87. No.102 is posed here in Swindon depot yard. D.A. Russell & D.M. Pemberton

Cheltenham & Gloucester has modified most of its dual-doorway Bristol VRs by eliminating the centre exit. The nearside aspect shows no sign of the former doorway, but the central staircase and revised seating layout do give the game away. No.5133 of the City of Gloucester division works the cross-city trunk route from Hucclecote. Allan Macfarlane

The picturesque setting of Marlborough High Street is the location of this view of Swindon & District 5527. This is a standard single-doorway version of the Bristol VR. K.R. Crawley

Cheltenham & Gloucester has been increasing its Leyland National stock by transferring examples from the related Midland Red South fleet. One of the native buses, though, is 3052, wearing Stroud Valleys colours. Now that Stroud's bus station is closed, kerbside bus stops are used again in the town, as they were until 30 years ago. David Stewart

Thirteen Leyland Nationals have been modernised by the company to what it calls National 3 or 3A standards, featuring a DAF engine, new entrance doors, general refurbishment and, in some cases, new heating to eliminate the roof pod. They are now numbered 301-313 and painted in a distinctive livery with grey relief. Cheltenham District 312 hasn't much room to manoeuvre at Gloucester bus station. Bristol Vintage Bus Group

1985 saw a major conversion of several Gloucester and Cheltenham town services to minibus operation, with Metro-named Ford Transits. Most are still on the same work, as shown by 642 in Cheltenham town centre. D.A. Russell & D.M. Pemberton

The follow-up choice to the original 16-seat Transit minibuses was the 20-seat Mercedes-Benz L608D, also converted for psv work by Alexander. No.654 is shown at Norwood Arms, Cheltenham. Colin Martin

A much more sophisticated type of minibus was chosen for more Cheltenham Metro routes, and also for the first to start in Swindon, namely the MCW Metrorider. One of these sleek 25-seaters is seen on Cheltenham's Promenade in the afternoon sun. Colin Martin

The Black & White fleetname generates memories for the older enthusiast of immaculate and distinctively-painted coaches heading all over the country from Cheltenham. The image disappeared under National Express white, but the name re-appeared in 1984 and became part of Cheltenham & Gloucester a year later. Although only ever on a handful of coaches, the name is still worn with pride and 2202 displays the current form of livery. D.A. Russell & D.M. Pemberton

CITY LINE - OVERGROUND

Bristol Omnibus Company Ltd, Enterprise House, Easton Road, Lawrence Hill, Bristol BS5 0DZ

Bristol Omnibus Company used to operate within an area that included towns now the territory of Badgerline and Cheltenham & Gloucester Omnibus Co.

The company's remaining area includes the Greater Bristol conurbation plus a number of tendered services that have been secured for routes outside this area and which are of a sparse nature.

The company was acquired from the National Bus Company by a consortium of the management team and Midland Red West in September 1987. In April 1988 Badgerline Holdings Ltd merged with Midland Red West Holdings Ltd, leaving both major operators working in Bristol in the same group. The Badgerline group now consists of Midland Red West, Eastern National, Thamesway, South Wales Transport, Bristol Omnibus (City Line), Brewers, United Welsh and Wessex Bristol), Western National and Badgerline itself.

City Line depots are located at Moravian Road, Kingswood; Easton Road, Lawrence Hill; Winterstoke Road, Ashton Gate and Muller Road, Horfield.

Fleet livery is yellow, red and blue, and minibuses carry City Dart fleetnames.

The Bristol VRs, which have formed the entire double-deck stock of both Muller Road and Winterstoke Road depots, are being replaced by new double-deckers. Typifying the VR is 5105, standing on The Centre in the afternoon sun.
Allan Macfarlane

Replacing the VRs are Leyland Olympians powered by Cummins engines. The bodywork is by Northern Counties, who last built for Bristol, or its associates, sixty years ago! Prior to taking over the 75 and 77/78 in the New Year, the buses have been employed on peak journeys to the Polytechnic or, as shown here by 9601, on Christmas 1992 season Park & Ride services.
Lee Turton

All of Lawrence Hill depot's double-deckers are Leyland Olympians with Roe single-doorway bodywork. They seat six more than the Bristol VRs. No.9554 shows off its lines after setting down at The Centre. Richard Eversden

Sixty-two Leyland Lynxes were placed in service in 1989/90, to renew the single-deck fleet. The second batch features electronic destination equipment within a revised fascia panel, as shown by 1650 in Westbury-on-Trym. Allan Macfarlane

Bristol CityLine now co-operates with Guide Friday to provide an open-top Bristol Tour during the high summer. Guide Friday has supplied one open-top Bristol VR — a single-doorway bus with its upstairs front windows still in situ — while CityLine supplies its two-door version, 5055. This also carries the Guide Friday livery, as can be seen. G.R. Mills

A very popular bus with her regular, peak-hour passengers is the 1966 Bristol Lodekka, C7262. Not only does her performance recall the days when things were a little less hurried, but her Tilling green livery reminds us of the times when colour schemes were more subdued. Allan Macfarlane

CityLine obtained 23 of the Robin Hood 19-seat Iveco minibuses that Badgerline had used when running its Salisbury and Portsmouth (Red Admiral) operations in 1987/88. CityLine runs them amid native Iveco/Dormobile and Mercedes-Benz 20-seaters and the few remaining Transits. Here, 7914 is dwarfed by two Olympians. D.A. Russell & D.M. Pemberton

DEVON GENERAL

Devon General Exeter Ltd, Belgrave Road, Exeter, Devon, EX1 2AJ
Torbay Bayline Ltd, Regents Close, Torquay, Devon.

Devon General Ltd is one of four fleets formed in January 1983 out of the Western National Omnibus Company Ltd. In 1970, Western National had taken over the Devon General Omnibus & Touring Co Ltd, now returning the new unit to virtually the same area as the old company; that is the South Devon Coast from the River Dart eastwards to Lyme Regis, bounded inland by Axminster, Taunton, Okehampton, Ashburton and Kingswear.

Devon General was the first of the National Bus fleets to be sold when a group of the company's managers, led by Harry Blundred, took over the company in August 1986.

The use of Ford Transit minibuses to replace conventional vehicles on town services was pioneered by NBC at Exeter from 1984 and Devon General have been in the forefront of this type of operation. This has continued to the extent that all big bus operation has now ceased on urban services and inter-urban routes also use midibuses. One open-top double decker remains.

Devon General became part of the Transit Holdings group in 1987. This group includes Thames Transit, Red Admiral and Blue Admiral.

Fleet livery is cream and dark red though minibus operation at Exeter is worked by three units within the Devon General Exeter operation. Each has its own fleet livery, red and yellow, blue and silver and two-tone green. The separate Torbay Bayline serves Newton Abbot, Torquay, Paignton and Brixham. The Brixham Coaches fleet is dark blue, while the Bayline unit in Torquay is red and cream.

As is well known, Devon General started the trend for major minibus operation in 1984 and has persevered with the idea to a far greater extent than almost anyone else. Not only were large numbers of Ford Transits bought new but several have been acquired from elsewhere. One such example is 590, which was new to Hampshire Bus, but obtained from United Counties. It looks perfectly at home at Torquay with its Carlyle-finished body. D.A Russell & D.M. Pemberton

No.935 is the one and only full-sized bus left in the Devon General or Bayline fleet. This alone works the Torbay open-top summer service and is seen passing Paignton Station in this view. It is the last of nine convertible Bristol VRs that were new to Torquay in 1977/78. *Barry Spencer*

Opposite upper **Having converted all of the local routes in its area to Transit operation, Devon General turned its attentions in 1988 to the interurban and rural services. They replaced the remaining full-sized buses and local coaches with a fleet of what they term Minicoaches. These are Mercedes-Benz 709Ds with attractive Reeve Burgess Beaver bodywork, accommodating 25 semicoach seats. No.49 displays route details for a Tiverton to Exeter service.** *BVBG*

Opposite lower **A Park & Ride operation is provided at Exeter with Ford Transits wearing blue, red and white livery. This photograph clearly shows the different ideas about window sizes which the body conversion companies had for this model. Leading bus 42 was finished by Mellor, while 737 was a Carlyle product.** *Barry Spencer*

NORTH DEVON RED BUS

North Devon Ltd, 39 St James Street, Taunton, Somerset, TA1 4AF

North Devon was formed on 1st January 1983 to take over the North Devon area of Western National Omnibus Co Ltd with depots at Barnstaple, Bideford and Ilfracombe. The area of operation covers the north Devon coast between Bude and Lynton and inland to Tiverton and Exeter.

The company was purchased by its management in March 1988 in a joint venture with the managers of Southern National and is now a subsidiary of Cawlett Ltd (a holding company). Contract services and some tendered services are worked from Exeter under the South Western fleetname and a group of services based on Tiverton use the 'Tiverton and District' fleetname. Vehicles used on the Ilfracombe to Bideford and Barnstaple service, which competes with Filer's, carry an Atlantic Blue name and blue livery.

Operational depots at Bideford and Ilfracombe have been closed and the Barnstaple site has moved to Coney Avenue. The Ilfracombe premises are still used as a paint shop and for the storage of vehicles and vehicles use the rear of a garage in Bideford as an outstation.

Fleet livery is red and white, but many of the fleet carry local liveries. Minibuses are yellow with two narrow red lines, though several still remain in older schemes.

The Dennis Dart new-generation midibus has achieved considerable sales success in London and other parts of the country, but is yet to make a major impact on the West Country. North Devon broke the ice in April 1991, though, with two examples carrying the distinctive Carlyle 40-seat body. They were specifically obtained for the Devon County supported service 308 from Barnstaple. The destination box is not pretty, but the clarity and fullness of display is commendable. Malcolm King

At its creation in 1983 out of the Western National Omnibus Company, North Devon's fleet included no Leyland Nationals. Recently, however, they have taken in several, generally to replace double-deckers. Most came from Southern National, but 2812 is a former Plymouth City Transport coach-seated conversion of a dual-doorway bus. It is seen trundling along The Strand in Barnstaple. Barry Spencer

7ft 6in wide Plaxton Supreme Express coachwork was chosen for the last delivery of Bristol LH6Ls for restricted rural services in Devon and Cornwall. North Devon still run four of them, though 3312 is seen on Bideford Quay on the trunk route from Appledore to Barnstaple. Barry Spencer

A form of the Bristol LH that seldom has appeared in NBC/ex-NBC fleets is the coach-bodied LHS model, with about 33 seats. North Devon chose this one when picking over the remains of the failed Country Bus Company of Atherington. No.3313 was new to Thistle of Doncaster and later ran for Silver Fox of Edinburgh during its travels. Graham Jones

North Devon took the chance to add more narrow Bristol LH types in 1990, when the Tyne & Wear Omnibus Company sold their ex-London Country LHSs. No.1612 is seen leaving Exeter (Bamfylde Street) on what is in effect a Tiverton & District service. Graham Jones

A solitary Dennis Dart was added to the fleet in April 1992. No.803 differs from 801/2 in carrying Wright Handybus bodywork. It is seen setting off from Barnstaple bus station. Barry Spencer

An 86-seat capacity attracted North Devon to a pair of East Lancs-bodied Leyland Atlanteans, chosen for South Western school contracts around Exeter. No.1211/2 came from Blackpool Transport and they are kept, with the other South Western stock, in Devon General's Exeter depot. Graham Jones

North Devon introduced the fleetname South Western when it took over the last Devon General big-bus workings on Devon County contracts round Exeter in April 1990. Two Bristol VRs were transferred from Southern National for the initial fleet, including 1162. Graham Jones

Among the last double-deckers to be displaced by Devon General were their seven Leyland/ECW Olympians. These passed to the associated North Devon and Southern National fleets, the former being found with the Tiverton & District branch. No.1811 passes through Cullompton in this scene. Barry Spencer

North Devon's rather abstract Little Red Bus livery has now been replaced by a very much simpler scheme . . . not red, of course, but yellow! Upon this are carried two red and crimson bands and Red Bus fleetnames. Robin Hood-converted Ford Transit 414 demonstrates the image at Barnstaple. Barry Spencer

Judging from their yellow livery, the new 29-seat Wright-bodied Mercedes-Benz 709Ds are minibuses. Seen at Ilfracombe bus station is 718 — note the Bournemouth registration, presumably obtained through Southern National's Weymouth engineering offices. Barry Spencer

PLYMOUTH CITYBUS

Plymouth Citybus Ltd, Milehouse, Plymouth, Devon, PL3 4AA

This company was formed in October 1986, the successor to Plymouth City Council's Transport Department, which had been providing a network of public transport for about 100 years. Local bus services are provided within the City of Plymouth area. Prior to 1986 a joint service agreement with Western National dated back to 1942. This allowed Western National vehicles to operate on certain services within the city boundary.

Since deregulation both operators have competed within the Plymouth area, and this has seen an exchange of work both on a commercial and tendered basis. The introduction of minibuses in 1986 reduced the conventional bus fleet, but provided an enhancement to a number of local routes.

In recent years, Plymouth has extended its coach fleet to 14 vehicles dedicated to Private Hire and CityCoach holidays. In 1991 Guide Friday of Stratford introduced the Plymouth open top tour of the city.

The depot and works are at Milehouse; fleet livery is black, white and red, with Plymouth Citybus names. Coaches carry Plymouth CityCoach names on a predominantly white livery with red and black trim.

Plymouth's first-generation minibuses were Dodge 50-Series models, with well-styled Reeve Burgess bodywork. These are now being replaced, but one of several which remain very much a part of the city's fleet is 80. Note the use of the bonnet for the advertising poster! Paul Burch

The new minibuses are Mercedes-Benz 709Ds, which also carry Reeve Burgess bodywork, but to the squarer Beaver design. No.205 demonstrates also the fact that these vehicles feature a white bonnet, carrying the fleetname, and that larger destination equipment is installed. The choice of Mercedes chassis was made as the result of evaluating a batch of four examples in 1990. Paul Burch

Midibuses seating around 40 may gain an important place in the fleet as direct replacements for double-deckers. The first nine are now in service and are Dennis Darts, with Plaxton Pointer bodies — an interesting contrast to the two alternatives with North Devon. A change to a light grey skirt is made with these. Seen at Brake Farm is the first of the batch, 101. Barry Spencer

Plymouth turned to East Lancs for the bodies on its final Atlantean intake, these also featuring Alexander windscreens at Plymouth's request. No.148 has one of the last registrations issued by Plymouth Vehicle Licensing Office before it closed in 1980. D.A. Russell & D.M. Pemberton

The two 1985 Volvo Citybus double-deck coaches, 175/6, have been superseded by new versions, so the originals have been re-equipped as buses. Apart from the installation of bus seats, the front end has been completely rebuilt, with Alexander-style curved windscreens replacing the previous large, squarer screens. Paul Burch

A high-quality coach fleet is maintained by Plymouth, under the fleetname CityCoach. No.346 is a Volvo B10M with Plaxton Paramount 3 coachwork and was photographed across the other side of England, at Spalding in Lincolnshire, during the Bulb Festival. G.R. Mills

The new Volvo/East Lancs double-deck coaches, 177/8, are on longer wheelbase chassis and seat 78 with a luggage boot, as opposed to 74 without a boot. The upper-deck front window is deeper and no destination screen is fitted. How will these be rebuilt when their time comes? No.178 is seen at Showbus, with a Badgerline version of this body beyond. G.R. Mills

SOUTHERN NATIONAL

Southern National Ltd, 39 St James Street, Taunton, Somerset, TA1 4AF

Southern National Ltd is one of the four fleets formed in January 1983 to take over the services of Western National Omnibus Co Ltd. Depots are at Bridport (Tannery Road), Bridgwater (East Quay), Taunton (Hamilton Road), Weymouth (Edward Street) and Yeovil (Reckleford Road), plus several outstations. The operating area of operation extends along the south coast between Lulworth and Lyme Regis running inland via Chard, Wellington, Porlock, the Bristol Channel coast north to Burnham-on-Sea, inland to Glastonbury, Frome, Wincanton, Sherbourne, Blandford, Wool and back to Lulworth, town services with minibuses are worked at Taunton, Yeovil and Weymouth with smaller operations at Chard, Dorchester and Bridport.

The company was purchased from National Bus by its management in March 1988, together with a share in North Devon Ltd, a holding company Cawlett Ltd being formed. The close relationship between North Devon and Southern National means that vehicle transfers and loans are commonplace, with an integrated fleet numbering system, though the operations remain separate.

Southern National, through Cawlett Ltd, has since acquired Brutonian of Bruton in Somerset, Smiths of Portland and Pearce, Darch and Wilcox of Martock. While the Brutonian fleet has now been absorbed both of the others retain their own identity.

Fleet livery is apple green and cream with minibuses yellow with two narrow green bands in the northern area whereas Weymouth vehicles used red and orange relief. There are several vehicles still in former schemes, some carrying 'Shuttle' names.

It took Southern National quite a time to develop a new livery to take the place of NBC leaf-green. The choice of apple-green and cream was well worth waiting for! This scheme is displayed by Bristol VR 1125. Curiously, the layout shown seems to be a 'Somerset' version of the livery, as VRs at Dorset depots feature a green roof and waistband! Graham Jones

Southern National and North Devon shared the batch of ECW-bodied Leyland Olympians offered by Devon General in 1990. Southern National's four are based at Weymouth, where we see 1812. Malcolm King

After nearly three years in store, Southern National re-instated former Bristol and Hants & Dorset LH6L 1634 in February 1990, complete with a repaint into the then-new apple-green and cream. Basically allocated to schools duties, the bus is seen in its home town of Bridport. Barry Spencer

The inevitable Ford Transit minibuses work town services throughout the region. This Robin Hood version in the yellow minibus livery has dual-green bands upon it for the Yeovil Shuttle network. Keith Grimes

The latest yellow-liveried minibuses are 29-seat Mercedes-Benz 709Ds. No.715 is one of the Wright-bodied examples shared with North Devon. It carries blue and orange stripes on the sides for operation at Weymouth. Malcolm King

After being illustrated in the last edition of this booklet working for North Devon's Tiverton & District wing, 1974-vintage Plaxton Panorama Elite bodied Bristol RELH 2421 was returned to Southern National and repainted in the cream and green livery, in June 1990. It is shown here at Weymouth. K.R. Crawley

THAMESDOWN TRANSPORT

Thamesdown Transport Ltd, Corporation Street, Swindon, Wiltshire, SN1 1DS

This company took over the bus operating department of Thamesdown Borough Council, who was the successor of Swindon Corporation Transport Department, in October 1986. Town services in Swindon form the main operation though tendered services for county councils extend the operating area into north and west Wiltshire, west Oxfordshire, west Berkshire and east Gloucestershire.

The private hire side has expanded and since 1980 has become a significant part of the fleet. In January 1992 a joint venture with Southampton Citybus took over the coach business of Kingston Coaches of Winterslow along with eighteen coaches. The Kingston Coaches, in a red and cream livery are based at Winterslow, near Salisbury.

Fleet livery is cream and aircraft blue, although coaches are in an aircraft blue, white, green and grey scheme. The works and depot are at Corporation Street, Swindon.

Thamesdown Transport has a great attachment for Dennis products and has, on several occasions, taken in modern examples from other operators. A case in point is 238, a former Derby City Transport Dominator, with Northern Counties bodywork, which fits very well into Thamesdown's fleet. G.R. Mills

Six Dennis Dominators were bought from East Staffordshire District Council/Stevensons of Uttoxeter in 1985, including 231. These, however, were the only East Lancs bodies in the Thamesdown fleet for a time. G.R. Mills

Thamesdown's standard choice of double-decker in the early 1980s was the Northern Counties bodied Dennis Dominator. Four batches arrived, each subtly different, and 63 is a member of the third intake. Thamesdown run some services well outside the borough boundary and 63 is seen ready to return home from Devizes. K.R. Crawley

After a break of four years, Thamesdown took one more batch of Dennis Dominators in 1990. These, however, have East Lancs bodies, of the pattern usually associated with coach seating — compare this with the examples with Badgerline, Plymouth and Yellow Buses. No.72 is seen on a service worked jointly with Swindon & District Bus Company. Malcolm King

The once-impressive ranks of Eastern Coach Works bodied Daimler/Leyland Fleetlines have been thinned now, as those without power-assisted steering have been retired. One of the final deliveries of the model, 203, is seen at the top of Fleming Way in the town centre. David Loxley

All full-sized single-deck buses in the fleet are Dennises . . . and all are secondhand. Seven Falcon H models, with Gardner 6HLXB engines and Duple Dominant Bus bodywork, were bought in 1987 from Leicester Citybus. The newest of them, 16, is seen in Cirencester. Malcolm King

The nine former London Transport DMS-class Leyland Fleetlines are still going strong and all are now in the current livery. This is displayed by 136 at the Fleming Way stops.
D.A. Russell & D.M. Pemberton

The ECW bodywork on Daimler Fleetline 175 was converted to open-top in 1985. The bus undertakes a variety of special duties, but here seems set to show off rolling Wiltshire countryside and the Avebury stone circle, on a run to Devizes.
G.R. Mills

The minibuses in the fleet are Renault-Dodge 50-Series. The first three were bodied by Reeve Burgess and therefore resemble the Plymouth versions. The remaining Thamesdown examples, including 412 seen here, have Northern Counties bodywork in which the bonnet is replaced by the bodybuilder's own frontal structure.
D.A. Russell & D.M. Pemberton

WESTERN NATIONAL

Western National Ltd, 21A Pydar Street, Truro, Cornwall, TF1 2AY

Western National Ltd is one of four new operators to take over from the Western National Omnibus Co Ltd in January 1983. The new Western National acquired the services in Cornwall and south Devon including a share in Plymouth Joint Services. The current operating area includes Cornwall and that part of Devon south and west of a line from the River Teign, through Teignmouth, Newton Abbot, Ashburton, Princetown and Launceston. Services for National Express, including Rapide, are also operated.

Western National Ltd was privatised in July 1987 when a consortium of Plympton Coachlines, Badgerline and banking interests acquired the company. Badgerline later bought out the Plympton Coachline and banking shares leaving Western National wholly owned by Badgerline Holdings Ltd. The business of Grenville of Camborne, including Bluebus, and Roberts Coaches of Plymouth were acquired in 1988. Both Grenville and Roberts fleet names are still used on vehicles allocated to those duties.

Fleet livery is cream and blue with red trim. Coaches are in Western National Coaches, Grenville, Roberts or National Express liveries as appropriate. A new livery is being introduced for all new vehicles and selective application to existing vehicles.

Depots are situated at Camborne, Plymouth (Laira Bridge), and St Austell. There are numerous outstations.

When requiring additional double-deck stock, Western National has taken advantage of the availability of Bristol VRs from other Badgerline Group members. This one, setting down at Truro, came from Badgerline itself in 1988. D.A. Russell & D.M. Pemberton

Four of the fifteen VRs that Badgerline had acquired from London Country Bus Services passed on to Western National in 1989. These are full-height models, so are numbered 933-6 to distinguish them. Their extra height is easily discernible and not just because the red band continues above the windscreen. At Penzance, 935 and 1144 demonstrate the difference. Graham Jones

Just repainted in the smart blue and cream livery is 1801, one of the eight Leyland-ECW Olympians. These all carry coach seats and a run on the X80 from Plymouth to Torquay with holidaymakers is putting their comfort to advantage. Graham Jones

The days are now numbered for the remaining short and narrow Bristol LHS 35-seaters in Cornwall. No.1558 has for some time been the only one at Camborne rather than Penzance. Graham Jones

Several modern 31-seat midibuses are now in the fleet, based on Mercedes-Benz 811D chassis. Carlyle built those delivered in 1990/91. They include 312 which is seen in a beautiful setting at Torquay. Barry Spencer

Four more Mercedes-Benz 811Ds, but with the distinctive Optare StarRider treatment, came into the fleet from Badgerline in 1991, initially on loan. No.330 features a red fleet number plate to signify allocation to Camborne, which is where it waits its next duty on the Truro service. Graham Jones

Six Leyland Lynx 51-seaters are the only full-sized single-deck buses in the fleet. They arrived just after the blue and cream livery had been introduced and carry these colours in a different layout to the other single deckers. No.203 is one of five based at Plymouth. Allan Macfarlane

'Welcome to Cornwall' it says on the side of this typical Mercedes-Benz L608D, turning at 'Snozzell' station. The psv conversions by the various bodybuilders were much the same in appearance, but this one, 80, is one of 16 equipped with 19 coach seats. D.A. Russell & D.M. Pemberton

The business of Grenville of Troon, near Camborne, was taken over in March 1988. Bus and coach activities retained the Grenville image for the rest of the year, but now the name is just confined to a selection of coaches. No.2453, a Leyland Leopard with Plaxton Supreme coachwork, is one of only three survivors from the acquired fleet. Barry Spencer

Clearly showing the narrow, 7ft 6in, width of the Plaxton Supreme Express coachwork of the company's final intake of Bristol LH6L models is this view of 3300, now the last survivor in the Western National division. It is seen at Compton, near Torquay, on the Devon County contracted service from Totnes. Barry Spencer

Having run the same service from Penzance to Mousehole every day since April 1977 — give or take a few! — this unusual Marshall-bodied Bristol LHS is just reaching the end of its career. PCV178R was new to local operator Harvey of Mousehole for the joint service with Western National. The service became Western National's own in 1988 and the bus was numbered 1566. It received a distinctive livery as a special gesture to Harvey's operations. This view shows it as many will like to remember it — turning at Mousehole Harbour in summer sunshine! Barry Spencer

WILTS & DORSET

Wilts & Dorset Bus Co Ltd, 2-8 Parkstone Road, Poole, Dorset, BH15 2PR

The Wilts & Dorset operation was purchased its management from the National Bus Company in June 1987 and has remained independent of any group. The original company started in January 1915 with a route from Salisbury to Amesbury and gradually expanded its area to serve most of Wiltshire, East Dorset and West Hampshire. The Southern Railway took an interest in Wilts & Dorset in 1930 and it became a Tilling subsidiary in that year, passing to the Tilling group in 1942 and to the BTC in 1948. Wilts & Dorset was merged, later absorbed, with Hants & Dorset under NBC control, but when Hants & Dorset was split in 1983 a new Wilts & Dorset company was created operating from depots at Blandford, Lymington, Pewsey, Poole, Ringwood, Salisbury and Swanage.

The Wilts & Dorset operating area stretches from Marlborough, Devizes, Warminster, Shaftesbury, Dorchester, Swanage, Lymington, Romsey, Andover and Hungerford. Local services reach Bath, Southampton and Swindon.

NBC red livery was used from 1983 but this has given way to a red, white, black and grey scheme applied in various bands.

Wilts & Dorset is famed among former NBC companies as never having taken any of its native Bristol VRs out of service. Indeed, it has added to them, by the purchase of three late model examples from Keighley & District in 1991. One of the latter, 3457, is seen here in Rolleston Street, Salisbury, just arriving after a run up from Southampton. Graham Jones

Above **Wilts & Dorset only bought five Leyland Olympians new, but has added a further 22, secondhand! One of six to be built for London Country Bus Services, with Leyland TL11 engines and only 72 seats in their Roe bodies, is 3919.** This style of body, with Alexander-pattern windscreen, is otherwise only seen in the Bristol, Badgerline and Cheltenham & Gloucester fleets. Barry Spencer

Upper Right **A somewhat squarer style of body is the East Lancs product found on Leyland Olympians 3924-6. These initially comprised an evaluation batch for Plymouth Citybus; they later passed to Stevensons of Uttoxeter, from whom Wilts & Dorset purchased them. No.3925 is about to load at Swanage Station for a picturesque run through the Isle of Purbeck and past the ruins of Corfe Castle.** Graham Jones

Right **Wilts & Dorset's one native batch of Olympians is fitted with coach seats in the ECW bodywork and wears a distinctive livery, featuring much more white. No.3901 is at Bournemouth, ready for a limited stop run to Salisbury on the X3 — a regular duty for members of this batch.** Graham Jones

A 1961 Bristol Lodekka convertible open topper was bought by Wilts & Dorset in 1992. It has been specially painted with an impression of a Southern Railway steam locomotive on the sides, in order to run in conjunction with the steam railway at Swanage. Numbered 4001, it was new as Bristol's 866NHT at Weston-super-Mare. This view shows it at Swanage Station. Phil Davies

Several open-toppers are provided by Wilts & Dorset for holidaymakers in the Poole and Bournemouth area, some even crossing aboard the Sandbanks-Shell Bay ferry. Most examples are Olympians with removable roofs, but there is also one Bristol VR. No.3351 is shown at Poole, on the 152 to Sandbanks which years ago was Hants & Dorset's 32, run by cream-painted open-top Bristol K5Gs. Graham Jones

Wilts & Dorset is one of few former NBC companies still running a batch of Bristol LH saloons. The newest is 3858, new to Bristol in 1980. It is seen here at Swanage on the service that will take it over the Sandbanks ferry, for which the front panel has been trimmed. Graham Jones

Wilts & Dorset has never gone in for the Ford Transit type of minibus and waited until 1987 before placing any small vehicles in service at all. Their exclusive choice has been the Metrorider, either by MCW or, nowadays, by Optare; the latter, furthermore, are 'stretched' versions. Seen here at Bournemouth is 2366 on route 105. This service was started in 1987 to echo Badger-Vectis journeys from Poole to Bournemouth and has since been projected to Christchurch and reaches Ringwood about every 90 minutes. K.R. Crawley

As a sign of respect for the operations of Verwood Transport after that concern was taken over by Wilts & Dorset, one Bristol VR was repainted into Verwood Transport's blue livery, with gold fleetnames. The bus is now numbered 4384 and is the newest VR in the low-mileage fleet. Interestingly, this bus has never worn red fleet livery, having carried overall advertising colours prior to the present blue scheme. Andy Gilmour

Wilts & Dorset co-operates with Guide Friday over the provision of a tour from Salisbury to Stonehenge. The two buses are Wilts & Dorset VRs — not open toppers in this case — which are painted in Guide Friday livery. At times, only one is required for the Stonehenge Tour, so the other takes its turn in ordinary service. In this scene at Blue Boar Row, 3332, seconded to city service 52, passes 3334, which is handling the Tour alone. Graham Jones

YELLOW BUSES

Bournemouth Transport Ltd, Mallard Road, Bournemouth, BH8 9PN

Bournemouth Transport Ltd is the successor to Bournemouth Corporation Transport Department and operates the majority of stage services for Bournemouth in an area extending from Poole to Christchurch along the south coast and inland to Holdenhurst, Throop and Kinson.

Deregulation saw several operators introduce competitive services in the area, several competing with Yellow Buses, but all have now ceased. In April 1992 Dorset Travel Services was acquired from its joint management and National Express ownership while new contracts for National Express services have been secured for the 1992/3 winter schedule.

Fleet livery is yellow with blue roof and skirt panels. The depot is in Mallard Road, Bournemouth.

The Yellow Buses fleet still contains around 50 Daimler or Leyland Fleetlines, carrying Alexander bodies with a pleasant 'traditional' look to them. The earliest are 18 years old — not unusual for Bournemouth — but 160 seen here, is one of the newer examples, with only 13 years behind it.
K.R. Crawley

Bournemouth's position as a major holiday centre with beautiful coastal scenery makes owning a fleet of open-toppers almost essential! Nine Fleetlines with Alexander bodies have removable roofs for the popular run along the top of the cliffs and round the Chines, from Sandbanks to Christchurch. No.139 pauses at Bournemouth Square while eastbound. K.R. Crawley

Bournemouth made the unusual choice of contracting Marshall of Cambridge to body its batch of early production Leyland Olympians. The result was certainly different from the customary Alexander look, as 182 shows. After years of loyalty to Atlanteans and Fleetlines, Bournemouth might have been expected to settle on their successor, the Olympians. This was not to be, though, and these 20 remain alone in the fleet. Bristol Vintage Bus Group

After dabbling with Volvo Citybuses, Yellow Buses has now turned to the Dennis Dominator chassis. The R-Type bodywork is not what it seems as it was built by East Lancs. This builder gives the option of an Alexander look-alike and the only safe way to tell is by the upstairs back window and the cab window framework. The electronic destination screen falls far short of supplying the same amount of information as Bournemouth's traditional displays. Malcolm King

The Yellow Coaches fleet of Plaxton-bodied Leylands and DAFs is augmented by five Volvo Citybus double-deckers, numbered 200-204. These have the characteristic East Lancs coach body, as found elsewhere in the South West. Bournemouth's, however, differ . . . as shown by 203, these feature windscreens of the BET pattern — the days of variety are not yet passed! Malcolm King

ABUS

Alan Peters, 104 Winchester Road, Brislington, Bristol BS4 3NL

Alan Peters was formerly an employee of one of the local large operators and, having been made redundant, decided to set up a competitive commercial service from Keynsham to Bristol. These operations commenced in April 1991. Initially, one vehicle operated on the regular commuter service, A49, that operates Monday to Friday, sometimes duplicated by a Bristol VRT from the Munden fleet of Crown Coaches.

Livery is cream and blue and the operating centre is at Crown Coaches garage at Freestone Road, St Phillips, Bristol.

Since deregulation there has been little competition in the Bristol area. An exception is the ABus service A49 from Bristol to Keynsham, which offers cheap fares on an all-day service. Former Thamesdown Fleetline 184 is used on this service and is seen near to the Crown garage in St Phillips where it is based. Geoff Mills

ARROW COACHES

Arrowfleet Contracts Ltd, 77-85 Church Road, Redfield, Bristol, BS5 9JR

W.G.Barrett commenced operations in 1975 having previously built up a sizeable vehicle hire fleet of cars, vans, trucks and minibuses. Caetano bodied Ford coaches and MAN midibuses formed the early fleet that was used on private hire and contract services. With the deregulation of licences for express services a route to London was introduced under the 'Ambassador' name and this is still in operation. The deregulation of stage services in 1986 resulted in Arrow being awarded several tendered services from Avon County Council and commercial services are also operated in the Bristol area.

In 1989, the Somerbus service 580 was acquired, establishing Arrow as provider of several tendered services in the Bristol area in addition to their private hire and contract service activities.

Services currently operated are tendered routes 508/9, 532/3, 558, 588/9 for Avon County Council and commercial services 80 and 89A.

The depot is at Church Road, Bristol, with a yard at Lawrence Hill railway station for vehicle storage. Fleet livery is white with brown and orange trim.

Arrowfleet PLC operate a number of tendered services for Avon County Council and have a mixed fleet of buses for use on these routes. Two Leyland Swifts with Wadham Stringer bodies are among the selection, this one having been demonstrated to People's Provincial before delivery. F67SMC is seen working the 589 from Oldland via Hanham to Bristol. Allan Macfarlane

The Optare Citypacer is not a common vehicle in the Bristol area. One of two in the Arrow fleet is seen at Bristol Centre (still known by older members of the population as 'The Tramways Centre') on route 508 which is the off-peak working of Cityline service 8 between Clifton and Temple Meads via Redland.
Allan Macfarlane

AXE VALLEY

Mrs F M Searle, Virtues Vineyard, Southleigh, Colyton, Devon, EX13 6JA

Mrs Searle started her first stage service in 1982 and now operates four services in the Seaton area. Of these, route 885, from Seaton through Colyton to Axminster, has the highest frequency with seven return journeys Monday to Saturday and two on Sunday afternoons. Route 899 runs from Sidmouth to Lyme Regis through Seaton, with five return weekday journeys, and town centre service 891 operates within Seaton and also provides occasional trips to Beer and Axminster.

Fleet livery is cream and red and the vehicles operate from Colyton.

Based at Colyford, Axe Valley operate tendered services for Devon County Council in the Seaton and Beer area. Private hire is also catered for and this unusual Volkswagen LT50, with Dixon Lomas designed body built by Made-to-Measure, advertises this fact. It is seen at the fleet's base at Virtues Vineyard, Southleigh. Barry Spencer

BAKERS

Bakers Coaches Ltd, 88 High Street, Weston-super-Mare, Avon, BS23 1HT

Charles Theodore Baker borrowed money from his brothers in 1889 to buy a pony chair with which he plied for hire on the promenade. The business prospered and expanded into cabs and broughams, and a funeral furnishing business.

In 1930 his son, John Nowell Baker, was taken into partnership as C T Baker & Son and in 1933 the first coaches were acquired for use on excursions and tours as well as private hire. During the Second World War the coaches were contracted out to Imperial Airways and normal coaching activities ceased until 1946 when operations again resumed and the fleet quickly expanded to nineteen vehicles. In 1953 the licences of Wessex Coaches, a Weston based tours operator, were acquired and the seafront site at 10 Beach Road was purchased.

In April 1959 the name was changed to J N Baker Ltd. Contract work for Somerset County Council added to activities from 1960 and the travel agency business 'Bakers Dolphin Travel' commenced in 1962. The latter now has 30 outlets throughout North Somerset and Avon.

In recent times the fleets of Waverley Coaches, Silver Queen at Weston, Fursland of Bridgwater and WEMS Coaches of Clevedon and Weston have been taken over adding to the vehicle strength. Operations include two express services to London; Continental and British tours; local excursions; school and commercial contracts; and tendered bus services for both Avon and Somerset County Councils.

The head office is at Weston, and there are depots at Locking Road, Weston and Bristol Road, Bridgwater. The current livery is white with blue, lime green and yellow bands on coaches, and mid blue with white relief for buses.

Baker's double-deck bus fleet is now composed entirely of Bristol VRTs. Four are Eastern Coachworks bodied and include one each from Maidstone & District and Crosville and two from United Automobile. All came via other fleets, in the case of UGR694R via Northumbria. Purchased mainly for use on school contracts, they are often used on private hire work, in this case a trip to Bristol Zoo. Allan Macfarlane

Beeline operate a number of services in Wiltshire, on one of which is seen a well looked after Bedford YMT with Duple Dominant bodywork. Less care, apparently, is taken with destination displays.
D. Loxley

BEELINE (Warminster)

R B Hayball, Bishopstrow Road, Warminster, Wiltshire, BA12 9HQ

The origins of Beeline can be traced back to W Cornelius of Warminster, trading as Melrose Coaches, who operated a Dennis 'G' Coach in 1928. Two 29-seat Bedfords passed to the Warminster Motor Co in 1953, the latter being acquired by Berridge & Sons in September 1957. The Beeline name was first used by Warminster Motor Company and this continues in use.

The work undertaken includes private hire, contracts, excursions and tours with stage services commencing following the award of tenders from Wiltshire County Council.

Services include market day journeys from Bishopstow to Salisbury; Chitterne to Warminster and Kingston Deverill to Warminster.

Fleet livery is red and white.

BERE REGIS

Bere Regis Coaches, 7 Bridport Road, Dorchester, Dorset, DT1 1RW

R.W.Toop commenced in 1929 with a 14-seat Ford bus working on services from Bere Regis to Dorchester, Poole, and Wareham. J.W.Ironside of Winfrith, who operated services between Winfrith, Dorchester, Wareham and Weymouth became a partner in 1930; the partnership using the 'Pioneer' fleetname.

Between 1936 and 1945 thirteen other operations were taken over and the first of five double deckers was acquired in 1947. The last of these were withdrawn in 1960 when the Dorchester to Poole service passed to Hants and Dorset. Following the death of the partners it was decided Bere Regis Coaches would operate as a trusteeship.

The fleet had a large variety of body types in use, especially in the 1950s and 1960s with fewer than 24 bodybuilders being represented. While the fleet strength reached 100 for a time this has recently declined. Today, stage operation covers most of south Dorset though many villages are visited by only one or two trips a week on market days. Tendered services for Dorset County Council are also worked in addition to Tours, Excursions and contract services.

The head office is at 7 Bridport Road, Dorchester and vehicles are housed at Bere Regis, Bridport, Dorchester, Hazelbury Bryan, Sherborne and Wimborne. Fleet livery is light brown with red trim.

BERRY'S

Cornishway West, New Wellington Road, Taunton, Somerset, TA1 6NA

C.G.Berry started his excursions and tours business in 1920 and it remained a small concern for many years. The 1939 fleet of three vehicles was requisitioned, but a secondhand Albion was obtained in 1943 and after the war slow expansion led to a new firm, Berry's Transport, being formed. This was a partnership between P.I.Berry and J.G.Hemming undertaking private hire, excursions, tours and contract work and gradual expansion led to a move to the premises at Taunton.

With the introduction of coach deregulation an express service to London commenced in 1987 and this now starts at Tiverton and picks up at Taunton (a feeder running from Wellington), and Bridgwater with two return services each day with a third run on Friday and Saturday. In addition, a large tours programme is operated, plus three commercial bus services Taunton to Wellington, Tiverton to Bridgwater and Taunton Station to Bishops Lydeard (West Somerset Railway link). Services from Taunton to West Fitzhead (Tuesdays) and Taunton Station to Bishops Hull (Tuesdays, Wednesdays and Fridays) are operated on tender to Somerset County Council.

The garage is at New Wellington Road, Taunton. While bus livery is red and orange, coach livery is white with red and orange stripes.

Berry's built up a fleet of Bristol VRs to furnish several services in the Taunton area in competition with Southern National, including two town routes, all of which used the 'BEAVERBUS' marketing name. Notable purchases were four from the fleet of the Atomic Energy Research Establishment at Harwell. The town services are no longer worked, but the B22 to Wellington is still operated and employs XAN431T which came via Roselyn of Par. Barry Spencer

BLANDFORD BUS COMPANY

Blandford Bus Company, 7 Eastleaze Road, Blandford Forum, Dorset, DT11 7UN

J.V.Cumming commenced operations in November 1988 with the purchase of an Eastern Coach Works bodied Bristol RELH from Scarborough and District. Stage services commenced in April 1989 with aid from the Rural Transport Development Fund. A Seddon Pennine VII, with Plaxton Supreme bodywork, was purchased to operate these market day services in the north Dorset area. Subsequently, the services from Melcombe Bingham to Blandford and Bere Regis to Blandford were taken over from Bere Regis and District Coaches.

In November 1991 a tender to operate the Milton Abbas to Dorchester service was gained on which a Bristol RESL is usually used. Eight routes are now operated of which only two are worked every day (except Sunday), the other six being provided on market days.

Fleet livery is white and blue with vehicles based at the Sunrise Business Park, Blandford and at Stanbridge.

Milton Abbas is the picturesque setting for former Merthyr Tydfil Bristol RESL6G NHB190M as it works on route 111 serving Dorchester from Blandford on Mondays to Saturdays. Steve Hursthouse

BROOKSIDE

T S, T F & J K Thomas, Brookside Garage, Relubbus, Penzance, Cornwall, TR20 4EN

Brookside started operation in August 1983 and operates a limited network of services in this western peninsula.

The main routes are Relubbus to Penzance, both direct and through Marazion, together with services to Truro, St Just, Penzance and Falmouth. Fleet livery in blue-grey with red and blue bands.

HJT39N is a much travelled Bristol LH. Having started life with Hants & Dorset, it spent some time operating in the North East of England before migrating south to Penzance. Brookside operate the 644 from Penzance to Relubbus via Marazion. Dave Took

CASTLEWAYS

Castleways (Winchcombe) Ltd, Castle House, Greet Road, Winchcombe, Gloucestershire, GL54 5PU

Trevor Fogarty started in Broadway as Tower Coaches during 1962. In January 1971 he took over Gilletts Coaches of Winchcombe, registering the business as a limited company, Castleways (Winchcombe) Ltd. Gilletts had shared the Cheltenham to Winchcombe service with both Kearseys Coaches of Cheltenham and the Bristol Omnibus Company. Castleways took over the running of these services and extended them northwards to Broadway and Willersey together with the service between Willersey and Evesham previously worked by Midland Red. Other services link Greet to Cheltenham and Winchcombe to Evesham and less frequent services reach Moreton in Marsh and Stratford-upon-Avon.

Fleet livery is black and Washington grey; the depot is in Greet Road, Winchcombe.

Castleways newest 'Bus' is this Optare Starrider bodied Mercedes-Benz 811D, seen in the usual immaculate condition that one expects of a vehicle in this fleet. Tesco's Store at Evesham is served by several of Castleways services. Colin Martin

Reeve Burgess bodied H383HFH has just had a wash prior to working a school contract. It is seen at Greet Road depot. Colin Martin

CIRCLE-LINE

Abbey Road, Monk Meadow Dock, Gloucester, GL2 6HU

Operations began in 1980 with two secondhand coaches. Business grew steadily and with emphasis on school contracts a fleet of double deckers was quickly built up. During the latter part of the 1980s the double-deck fleet, around a dozen strong, was particularly distinctive as the vehicles carried all-over advertisements – unusual for an independent operator. The opening of a new Superstore at Quedgeley on the southern outskirts of Gloucester brought a contract to provide a half-hourly link with the City Centre together with shoppers' services from many rural areas of the county. When this contract ceased, in 1990, Circle-Line turned its attention to local service work and built up a network of commercial services within and between Cheltenham and Gloucester in competition with Cheltenham & Gloucester. D.P.Ashby, the surviving partner of the original operation, formed a limited company at a time when the fleet strength was 40. A new livery of Brunswick green and cream was introduced at the same time.

Following a period of intense competition Western Travel, the holding company of Cheltenham and Gloucester, purchased a minority stake in Circle-Line and the competing services were withdrawn. Circle-Line continues to operate several tendered services in Cheltenham and some rural services south from Gloucester; it also operates a Saturday Park-and-Ride service in Cheltenham. A recent contract has led to the purchase of several vehicles fitted with wheelchair lifts, including a Leyland Leopard.

While a few double deckers retain all-over advertisements, most are now in the green and cream livery as are the bus-seated Seddons. The Leyland Cubs and Ford Transit are white with green trim and coaches are generally white with various stripes.

The large number of Bristol VRTs acquired for the competitive services in both Gloucester and Cheltenham have now been reduced in number since the change of ownership, but quite a few are needed for use on contracts including three which carry lettering for the Cheltenham Park-and-Ride service, namely LEU266P, PHY693S and the bus seen here, LEU267P. Colin Martin

CLAPTON COACHES

Clapton Coaches Ltd, Number One, Haydon Estate, Radstock, Bath, BA3 3RD

Mr & Mrs Chivers formed Clapton Coaches in 1978. Operations include private hire, holiday tours and stage services both commercial and tendered. Services are operated for Somerset, Wiltshire and Avon County Councils with Clapton vehicles now working to Swindon, Chippenham, Devizes, Trowbridge, Melksham, Bath, Weston-super-Mare, Shepton Mallet, Radstock, Street and Bristol.

Livery is white with blue lettering and lining.

Clapton Coaches have been successful with the winning of tenders for services in Avon, Somerset and Wiltshire, which require a sizeable fleet of mini and midibuses. A secondhand acquisition in 1991 was this Optare Starrider. The 666 is a one journey per weekday route from Bristol to Radstock via Clutton, Paulton and Midsomer Norton. Lawrie Bowles

COTTRELL'S

B N & E R Cottrell, Mill End, Mitcheldean, Gloucestershire, GL17 0HP

This family-owned business based on the village of Mitcheldean dates back to the nineteenth century. The earliest recorded charabanc is a Model T Ford of 1921 and the first bus was a Chevrolet, purchased new in October 1926, with another Chevrolet being added in 1927, a GMC in 1928 and a Star Flyer in 1929. These vehicles were used to establish several stage services, the main one linking Ruardean and Gloucester – still the main route operated today. With a two hourly frequency it combines with a Cinderford to Gloucester service to give an hourly service between Mitcheldean and Gloucester. Services also work to Cinderford and Ross-on-Wye plus some less frequent local routes. Double-deck buses have now been used for more than forty years; the current fleet includes one purchased new.

The office and garage is at Mill End, Mitcheldean and fleet livery is maroon and cream.

Mainstay of the double-deck content of the fleet in recent years are two MCW Metrobuses from the Greater Manchester fleet, which are used on the trunk Cinderford and Ruardean services. GBU6V prepares to reverse at Gloucester Bus Station. Allan Macfarlane

CROWN

L C Munden & Sons Ltd, 6/7 Freestone Road, St Phillips, Bristol, Avon BS2 0QN

Len Munden started trading in 1948 at Bridgwater, taking over the fleet of Harris Motors (Airbourne Coaches) with five vehicles.

The Bridgwater business ceased in 1953 when Mr Munden moved to Bristol, bringing a Leyland Cheetah once in the South Midland fleet with him; Leylands have been a favoured type ever since. Mr Munden became well known locally as a boxing promoter, and was known for being one of the only PSV drivers in the country to have only one arm.

The fleet gradually expanded with contract services and private hire work and in 1977 Empress Coaches, together with subsidiary Monarch Coaches, was acquired. This included a garage at Speedwell, Bristol and gave a base for Crown with large catchment area for the excursions and tours licences acquired with Empress. Since the 1970s several Leylands have been given a new lease of life by being rebodied.

In the initial tendering of services by Avon County Council several off-peak stage journeys that combine schools contracts in their schedules, were obtained.

Fleet livery is red and cream for coaches but the bus fleet is in a red and white scheme, the double deckers having a similar style to that used by Badgerline.

The depot and office is at Freestone Road, St Phillips.

The four former London Country via Badgerline highbridge Bristol VRs give yeoman service on contract as well as tendered services in the Bristol area. The 620 Bath to Chipping Sodbury route was however lost recently. Geoff Mills

DAWLISH COACHES

Shutterton Industrial Estate, Dawlish, Devon, EX7 0HN

R.C.L.Tomlinson started operating in May 1954 when he purchased an Opel Blitz 26-seat coach that had originated with Wessex of Bristol. Contract and private hire was undertaken and in 1956 a limited company was formed. Currently, contracts and private hire still form an important part of the work. Eight executive coaches are in service and are mostly used on Continental Tours. Two contract 'vintage' vehicles, two double deckers and ten other coaches form the fleet. A town service is operated in Dawlish under a DevonBus contract as are a Wednesday and Friday service linking Dawlish with Trago Mills that passes through Teignmouth, Poolsear and Combehead.

Fleet livery is white with red and blue relief and the vehicle base is at Shutterton, Dawlish.

Dawlish Coaches are better known in the west country for their coach fleet, but they maintain a local service at Dawlish and several tendered routes for Devon County. Three Fleetlines are currently owned including two Roe-bodied examples from the York Pullman fleet, the newer of which is seen at the Strand, Torquay on a school run. Barry Spencer

DEVON SERVICES

B T Smith & J A Dark, 57A Torquay Road, Paignton, Devon TQ3 3DT

Devon Services started in 1985 operating private hire from a base at Totnes and now also operate tendered services for Devon County Council. Eight services are operated in the Totnes and Torbay area on which a number of single deck service buses are used.

Fleet livery is white and mid blue, coaches carry AB Coaches names on a white and red livery.

A number of buses are operated, mostly based on Bristol chassis to operate tendered services in the Totnes and Torbay areas. An interesting vehicle acquired in 1990 from Teesside was this LH6L which was ordered by Wigan but was delivered to Greater Manchester PTE. The flat front was fitted when new at the request of Wigan after the later curved front design had been introduced as standard. BNE767N also worked for Silcox of Pembroke Dock from 1982 to 1987. Barry Spencer

DUKE'S TRAVEL

K G & P K Bevan, Ferndale, Edge End, Coleford, Gloucestershire.

After two years in partnership with M.M.Griffin (trading as Lydbrook Coachways), K.G.Bevan set up Duke's Travel with two coaches in 1976. For some years the business centred around contract and private hire work and excursions but since 1989 a number of local services have been operated in the Coleford area, the most significant being from Coleford to Ross. Saturday services run from the Lydbrook area to Gloucester.

The depot is in Laker's Road, Berry Hill, near Coleford, while fleet livery is white and green with an orange band.

Seen at Gloucester on the Saturday run from Coleford is MYO486X, a Leyland Leopard with Wadham Stringer body acquired in 1991 from the Ministry of Defence, an unusual source for vehicles to be used as PCVs. BVBG

Coleford Square is the location of this view of H556TUG, a Mercedes-Benz 709D bodied by Dormobile and purchased new in 1990. Although to coach specification, it is regularly used on local stage services in the Coleford and Ross-on-Wye areas.
Colin Martin

DURBIN

Merebrook Farm, Tockington Lane, Almondsbury, Avon, BS12 4EB

The name Durbin has been associated with coaching in the Bristol area since 1951 when A.W.Durbin in partnership with D.Couchman started in business at Patchway. This partnership was dissolved in 1954 when Couchman started up on his own as 'Coachways' while Mr Durbin continued and in 1954 acquired a coach from Northern Roadways of Glasgow which inspired the new fleetname 'Western Roadways'. Unusual vehicles for those days, including four Caetano bodied Bedford VALs, formed part of the fleet. Durbin sold out to Turners Coaches of Bristol in 1979 by which time twenty-eight coaches were in use.

Some five years later, 1984, Mr Durbin's son Roger started a coach company operating contract and private hire services which has evolved into tendered stage operation since deregulation. Four commercial routes, plus eleven services on tender to Avon County Council are operated in addition to numerous school services.

Vehicles are kept at Station Road, Patchway. Fleet livery is orange for buses, and white, red and orange for coaches.

The winning of Avon tenders for off-peak services and contract work required the use of double deckers and like a number of smaller fleets, Durbin's chose the Bristol VR. Four are now in the fleet including this dual-door bus from the Cityline fleet. As this was being written a new livery of overall orange with 'ORANGE' fleetnames was being introduced. Roy Marshall

EAGLE

J H & A H Ball, Fireclay House, Netham Road, St George, Bristol, Avon, BS5 9JR

Herbert Ball started in business in 1926 hiring out bicycles for a penny-an-hour from converted stables in Goulter Street, Barton Hill, and by 1927 a model T Ford truck was in use with the cycle business during the week and with seats and a canopy fitted as a charabanc at weekends.

The hiring of this vehicle led to the purchase of a dedicated charabanc and by the outbreak of war in 1939 eight coaches were in use for excursions, tours and private hire. Mr Ball died in 1941 and his widow continued the business being joined by her son in 1952.

In 1983 the operation of Princess Mary Coaches, with four vehicles, was taken over with a garage at 152 Soundwell Road. This was used by Stevens until 1985 and in 1986 a move was made from the Goulter Street premises to a new yard and office block in Netham Road.

The new contracts gained called for stage carriage vehicles and several have passed through the fleet since then, often in ASDA superstore livery, a livery that has also been applied to some coaches. Several Avon County Council services are operated and for these several minibuses have been acquired. The fleet currently numbers nearly thirty vehicles, and although a variety of vehicle types have featured in the fleet, Bedfords and Leylands have been predominant, though latterly DAF chassis have been favoured for coaches.

Fleet livery is white with yellow and orange stripes. The double decker, once in ASDA livery of white with green/blue lettering, is now overall white.

Seen in Eagle's white bus livery is E300OMG, a Mercedes 609D bodied by Reeve Burgess working on one of Eagle's evening services tendered from Avon County Council. Roy Marshall

FILER'S

R J Filer, Slade Lodge, Slade Road, Ilfracombe, Devon, EX34 8IB

The Filer family operated a taxi business in the town for several years and in March 1970 a PSV minibus was purchased and then a series of 29-seat coaches, with the first full sized coach arriving in 1980. Works and school contract services were the mainstay of the operation until 1986 when the local bus operator, North Devon Ltd, reorganised its services using minibuses, and the through route from Ilfracombe to Barnstaple was no longer served directly. Filers introduced a 'Rail Link' service to Barnstaple railway station and this soon expanded to restore the former Western National service 301, from Ilfracombe through Barnstaple to Bideford, to an almost hourly frequency. In 1988 the Bideford to Hartland service on contract to Devon County Council was won and the 301 workings were incorporated into those of this service. Currently Devon services 301-5/19 are worked, 302-5 being less frequent and based on Ilfracombe.

Former London Buses Daimler and Leyland Fleetlines and a former Alder Valley Leyland Olympian form the bus fleet and several coaches are also to be found on service. The fleet livery is yellow and blue. The garage and office are in a former quarry area off Slade Road, Ilfracombe.

Former London Transport DMS2030 is seen on Filers service 301 from Ilfracombe to Westward Ho! or Woolacombe, which competes with North Devon (Red Bus). Malcolm King

FORD

P I, A P & A Ford, Rylands Garage, St Anns Chaple, Gunnislake, Cornwall, PL18 9HW

The Ford family are successors to the old established firm of Watson of Gunnislake. A partnership of Ford and Watson was formed in 1957 since which time the operation of excursions and tours has continued to the present day.

Currently, two stage services are operated in the Tavistock district on contract to Devon County Council. Fleet livery is white and red with the depot located in Gunnislake.

Fords operate the Tavistock to Harrowbarrow via Gunnislake service and Bedford YRQ/Duple Dominant HVJ146N carries advertising lettering to promote the service. It is seen at Tavistock.
John Hobbs

FOSSEWAY

J V Pickford, The Post Office, Grittleton, Chippenham, Wiltshire, SN14 6AP

Mr Pickford developed a group of tendered bus services in north west Wiltshire and the eastern part of Avon. Communities served are Westbury, Corsham and Yate with services reaching Bath, Wotton-under-Edge, Melksham and Trowbridge. Town services are provided at Bradford-on-Avon and Chippenham, Trowbridge, Westbury and Corsham and at Yate in Avon.
   Minibuses, in a livery of dark blue and white, are used on these services.

Fosseway have built up a large fleet of minibuses for use on the many routes operated in north west Wiltshire and north east Avon. Ford Transits cast off by former NBC fleets are a feature represented by the ex-Alder Valley bus C336RPE on the Trowbridge service at Bath Bus Station.
Bristol Vintage Bus Group

HOPLEY'S

B Hopley, Sunic, Rope Walk, Mount Hawke, Truro, Cornwall, TR4 8DW

Hopley's operate services into Truro from the villages between St Agnes and Redruth, near the north Cornwall coast; occasional journeys also work through the village of Wheal Rose. These services were previously undertaken by Carter Brothers and it is normal to see the Bedford-Duple bus on this work.

In addition to this service work, a small fleet of coaches is used on contract and tours work. The fleet livery is white and red.

Hopleys operate Cornwall County Council tendered service 286 from Truro to Mount Hawke and NNK808P, a Duple bodied Bedford YRT, is seen on this service at Porthowan which is served on Wednesdays and Fridays. Roy Marshall

KILMINGTON

Mrs M P M Hutchings, Jay Bees, Bim Bom Lane, Kilmington, Axminster, Devon, EX13 7SL

Mrs Hutchings was the Honiton manager for Gourds Coaches of Newton Abbot and later became Managing Director and partner.   In May 1988 this partnership dissolved and Mrs Hutchings started Kilmington Coaches with just four minibuses.

In four years this has grown to a fourteen-vehicle fleet and a number of tendered services are run for Devon County Council. These are mainly in the Honiton area and serve Sidmouth, Taunton, Seaton, Axminster, Cullompton, Chard and Exeter, several on market days only.

Former Marton of West Drayton B440WUL is at Exeter Bus Station having worked a Friday journey from Kilmington and Honiton, typical of the nine services worked in the Axminster, Honiton, Seaton and Sidmouth areas. Barry Spencer

MAYBURY'S

B H & C Maybury, Creech Hill House, Cranborne, Wimborne, Dorset, BH21 5PN

Having operated coaches at Souldern in Oxfordshire for a number of years the Maybury's moved to Cranborne in 1975 and established a small coach hire business in that town. In 1984 they commenced operation on the London Sightseeing Tour in central London, being one of the 'big four' on this tour.

Several contract services are operated from Cranborne, including Wiltshire County Council tendered route from Fordingbridge to Salisbury with four daily return journeys on weekdays together with several contracts from Hampshire County Council including one from Rockley Sands to Sandhurst through Poole, seasonally operated with open-top buses.

Fleet livery is white with light blue and orange stripes while the depot and office are at the Cranborne address.

Double deckers in Maybury's current fleet include four former London Transport DMSs, two similar buses which started life with South Yorkshire, and one Bristol VR. AUD463R is seen at the Triangle Bournemouth. Note the painted-on Bristol VR badge. Graham Jones

OAKFIELD TRAVEL/ STANBRIDGE & CRICHEL

T C Greenslade, Sunrise Park, Higher Shaftesbury Road, Blandford Forum, Dorset, DT11 8ST

Oakfield Travel started to run local bus services in 1986 when the Sturminster Newton to Blandford Forum tendered service was awarded by Dorset County Council. Prior to this only contract and private hire work had being undertaken.

In 1989 the proprietors of Oakfield Travel purchased the Stanbridge & Crichel Bus Co from Barry Newsam of Barry's Coaches, Weymouth. The Stanbridge operations have been kept separate and operate as before including local services in the Wimborne and Cranborne areas taken over from Hants & Dorset Motor Services in 1980. The former Rossmore Bus Company service acquired by Stanbridge is also maintained.

The Oakfield garage and office are at Sunrise Business Park, Blandford, while the Stanbridge & Crichel garage and office is on the B3078 at Stanbridge.

Seen at Bournemouth taking a break is KDW706P, an East Lancashire bodied Bristol RESL6L new to Merthyr in 1975. It has worked the Saturday 303 from Blandford and Sturminster. Like Maybury's VR, the Bristol RE badge has been painted on. Roy Marshall

PROUT BROTHERS

O M Prout, Trelawny Garage, Port Isaac, Cornwall, PL29 3SB

The Prout family have been involved with road transport since the last century and by 1900 a horse drawn taxi service had been established at Port Isaac. Stage services to Camelford and Wadebridge were started in the 1920s and a fleet of hire cars and taxis maintained, several of the hire cars being PSV licensed.

The Port Isaac to Camelford commercial service is operated only on school days; the 255 service through Polzeath, Rock and St Minver to Wadebridge has four through journeys Monday to Saturday plus one short journey from Wadebridge to Polzeath.

Fleet livery is beige and green and the depot is located on the B3267 in Port Isaac. The office is at Trelawny Garage (a commercial garage and filling station) in the centre of Port Isaac.

Apart from one school service between Port Isaac and Camelford, Prout Brother's sole stage carriage service is a Cornwall County supported route from Port Isaac, round the coast via Polzeath, to Wadebridge. HAF430N, a Bedford YRT with Duple Dominant Express coachwork, is seen passing through Polzeath on such a journey. Barry Spencer

PULHAM'S

Pulham & Sons (Coaches) Ltd, Station Road, Bourton-on-the-Water, Gloucestershire, GL54 2EN

Pulham began operations in 1880 with a horse drawn carriers cart, motor buses being introduced in the 1920s when regular services from the original base at Naunton to Cheltenham were started. In the following decade services were extended to Bourton-on-the-Water, Stow-on-the-Wold and Moreton-in-Marsh. War work at Little Rissington provided considerable expansion of services in the area for the workers. This network of routes was expanded in the early 1960s when A.H.Kearsey's operation was taken over, adding a Cheltenham to Moreton-in-Marsh service and in 1968, Miles of Guiting Power, was acquired along with further stage services. The latest acquisition is Luxury Coaches of (Stow) Ltd which provide nine vehicles and further services.

These takeovers have given Pulham's a comprehensive cover of services in the Cheltenham, Bourton and Moreton-in-Marsh area.

The depot is at Station Road, Bourton, while fleet livery is cream and red. Despite all the stage carriage routes operated, only coach bodied vehicles are owned, though many are based on the erstwhile 'Grant' specification.

The Pulham's fleet contains many coaches bought new, but the opportunity is occasionally taken to buy suitable coaches secondhand. In 1991, three 1983 Leyland Tigers with Plaxton Paramount bodywork, similar to some already in the fleet, were bought from Reading Transport. These included RMO204Y, seen here on The Downs in Bristol, exemplifying Reading's distinctive destination screen, which would be useful on Pulham's own stage services. Colin Martin

RED BUS SERVICES

R M Holladay (Red Bus Services), Sandpiper, Honiton Road, Clyst Honiton, Exeter, EX5 3AN

In 1981 Mr Holladay worked as a seasonal driver/conductor with Devon General and for most of 1982 was unemployed. However, as an old vehicle enthusiast he used his time to restore a number of preserved vehicles including a former Devon General Albion Nimbus.

He obtained a certificate of Professional Competence after a correspondence course and was granted an operators licence and planned to run two services within Exeter. His application for these routes was refused after several objections. Devon General later introduced services to cover some of Mr Holladay's proposed routes.

At about the time East Devon Council had been selected as a trial area for deregulation of stage services and with the help of the County Council, Red Bus Services started two Saturday services to Exeter, one from Aylesbeare and Tipton St John, with the other from Feniton, Talaton and Whimple. Whimple was at this time the home base of Red Bus Services.

Expansion has continued and several tendered services have been secured from Devon County Council, with the fleet expanding accordingly. Services from Sidmouth to Honiton, and Ottery-St Mary and from Ottery-St Mary to Axminster are the main routes. Other, less frequent routes serve Talaton and nearby villages. Fleet livery is dark red and cream.

The immaculate Red Bus Services fleet, which has always contained much to interest the enthusiast, has conceded to present-day trends and bought a midibus, new! J844NOD is a 33-seat Wadham-Stringer bodied Mercedes-Benz 811D, seen passing Sidmouth thatched cottages on the Friday-only 382. Note the particularly clear destination display, typical of this firm, yet in sharp contrast to many on contracted stage duties. Barry Spencer

ROSELYN COACHES

L J & W B Ede, Middleway Garage, Par, St Austell, Cornwall, PL24 2JJ

Roselyn Coaches started to operate stage services when two school services were taken over from Hambly of Pelynt. Further stage services were acquired from Duchybus of Lostwithiel in 1980 though these were lost on tender to Western National in 1986.

Currently two services are worked: the 271 to Plymouth from St Austell through St Balzey, Par and Lostwithiel on three days a week, and the 270 Par to St Austell service with twelve return journeys on weekdays, four of which continue from Par to Fowey. Two services are operated to Mid Cornwall College of St Austell, one from Pelynt and the other from East Looe, as route 227.

Other activities include a summer park-and-ride service at Mevagissey, excursions, tours, both UK and European, and works contract services.

The fleet has always included an interesting selection of secondhand double-deck buses as well as coaches; minibuses being introduced during 1991. Bus livery is light and dark green while coaches carry gold stripes on a similar scheme.

There's no mistaking the duties expected of URD889N by the lettering applied to the bodywork! This is a Willowbrook-bodied Bedford, acquired after 14 easy years as a well-maintained staff bus for the Atomic Energy Research Establishment in south Oxfordshire — a frequent source for Roselyn buses. This picture was taken at St Blazey and the 'Service' concerned is their principal route, between Fowey, Par and St Austell.
Barry Spencer

Of much more up-to-date styling, although less than two years newer than URD889N, is NNK809P, with Duple Dominant Bus bodywork. Sixty-six passengers can be seated through the use of triple seats on one side of the gangway. This Bedford YRT was photographed at Bethel, 11 minutes from the St Austell terminus.
Barry Spencer

RYAN

M J Ryan, Watersmeet Cottage, Langridge, Bath BA1 8AJ

Mr Ryan purchased a Bedford WTB from City Coaches of Bath in 1949 to establish his private hire business at Marshfield. This business slowly expanded and by 1966, when he sold this business to Godwins of Marshfield, three coaches were in use.

When Mr Ryan restarted a business he purchased a Bedford minibus and gradually further minibuses were added to the fleet until 1985, when a larger vehicle, a Bristol LHS was purchased. For the 1989 Summer season three open-top double deck buses were placed in the fleet for competition with Badgerline on the Bath City Tour. A fourth open-top was added in 1990 and a further added in 1991. Private hire work expanded and tendered services for Avon County Council have been secured. Currently two such services are worked, Bath to Doynton and Marshfield plus the Friday return trip from Bath to Tadwick.

Livery is white with blue and red stripes for coaches; the open top double deckers are dark red with white relief and large Citytour names in white.

The garage is at Locksbrook Road, Bath.

Ryan's operate an open-top tour of the fine city of Bath, covering a route that differs slightly from the Badgerline Bath Tour. However, like the latter fleet, Bristol VRs are employed (among other makes in Ryan's case), one of which is NUD106L, which had been converted initially for the Oxford city tour, by South Midland. The coach seats downstairs are a reminder of the vehicle's original duties. G.R. Mills

SAFEWAY

Miss V Gunn MBE, North Street Garage, South Petherton, Somerset, TA13 5PA

In March 1928 G.Gunn started operating a stage service from Yeovil to Crewkerne using a 20-seat Dennis bus, operations gradually expanded until by 1939 the fleet numbered seven. Mr Gunn and his brother ran the fleet at this time, Miss V Gunn acting as conductress. In 1978, when Mr Gunn died, Miss Gunn took over.

Bedford OWBs were added to the fleet during the Second World War and Bedfords were a common choice for many years, though by the 1970s Leylands were being purchased as the standard chassis type. In June 1979 one of Safeway's main rivals for fifty years, Hutchings & Cornelius, also of South Petherton, were taken over with four vehicles being added to the fleet.

Safeway's main services operate from Yeovil to Ilminster, Crewkerne and South Petherton and from Crewkerne to Taunton. Private hire, contracts, tours and excursions are also operated from the North Street Garage which also houses the office. Fleet livery is red, dark red and cream.

Now completing 20 years service with Safeway is RYA676L, a Leyland Leopard with BET-style Willowbrook bodywork. It is now rare to find still in service secondhand machines of this pattern from former BET fleets, so the two originals with Safeway are the more interesting for that. Both the company's principal routes link South Petherton and Crewkerne with Yeovil, but by totally different ways. P.D. Moth

SOMERBUS

Somerbus Ltd, The Triangle, Paulton, Bristol, Avon, BS18 5LE

Somerbus Ltd commenced stage operations in March 1988 on Avon County Council tendered service 565 from Hartcliffe to Broadmead. This continued until March 1989 after which the service was operated commercially as service 80 until the route was sold to Arrowfleet in November 1989. Since then various tendered services have been operated on behalf of Avon County Council, currently numbering eight routes plus two schools services. The most intensive are the circular 511 route from Baltic Wharf to Bristol centre which has a frequency of 30 minutes, and the three-vehicle route to Clevedon through Portishead. Other less frequent routes include works services to Cadbury's Somerdale factory and early morning journeys on the 554/555 service.

Vehicles are kept at Bishopsworth, Bristol and the fleet livery is white and yellow with red Somerbus names.

Somerbus have successfully tendered for several Avon County services since 1986, both in their home district around Norton-Radstock and in and around Bristol city. The 747/748 is an hourly service from the east side of Radstock, through Welton, to Paulton. On the service is one of two Dodge S56 minibuses, with severe-looking Northern Counties bodies, bought from Greater Manchester Buses. Neil Jennings

STREAMLINE BUSES

Streamline Buses (Bath) Ltd, Station Road, Lower Weston, Bath, Avon, BA1 2DY

Streamline Buses was started by Streamline Taxis of Bath to compete for tendered services from Avon County Council in the Bath area, a number of which have been secured and operated. Currently, minibus routes 720/1 are operated along with country services to Camerton, Glastonbury, Midsomer Norton and Radstock. The country routes are all off-peak timings of regular Badgerline routes.

The livery is white with red and black lines and lettering.

Streamline owns several minibuses for use on their Avon County funded services within and from Bath. G229EOA is an Iveco 49.10, with the Carlyle Dailybus 2 body — more than merely a bread van conversion (just!).
Bristol Vintage Bus Group

Other Streamline minibuses are Freight Rover Sherpas, which have rather ungainly bodies, converted from the factory high-top van by Made-to-Measure. D195LRJ is seen on Broad Quay in Bath.
Bristol Vintage Bus Group

SWANBROOK

D J, K J & J A Thomas, St Margaret's Road, Cheltenham, Gloucestershire, GL50 4DS

The late Mr W J Thomas, a vehicle dealer, entered the bus business in October 1960 with the acquisition of a small taxi and minibus firm in Gloucester. The present partnership was formed in 1989 upon the death of W.J.Thomas. Called Swanbrook after its original owning partners, Messrs Swann and Brook, this operation has grown into one of Gloucestershire's principal bus and coach operations. Although no longer as numerous, double-deck buses still feature in the fleet. They are normally to be found on schools and works contracts, though they still perform occasionally on stage services.

Swanbrook commenced stage services in 1974, taking over the Gloucester to Tewkesbury service from Cathedral Coaches of Gloucester. In 1978 the Gloucester through Saul to Arlingham, service was acquired from Ladvale of Dursley. A further expansion took place in 1981 in the wake of retrenchment by the Bristol Omnibus Company.

Miles' Cotswold Coaches of Andoversford was acquired in 1980, and Carterton Coaches the following year. This provided an outpost in neighbouring Oxfordshire and about the same time a depot was also opened at Charfield. The Charfield depot closed in 1989 and the operation was sold to its management in 1992, together with 11 vehicles.

All Swanbrook vehicles now operate from the original depot at Golden Valley, Staverton, on the western outskirts of Cheltenham.

Services include Arlingham, Frampton and Quedgeley to Gloucester; Gloucester to Tewkesbury and some recently acquired contracted journeys in the Tewkesbury and Evesham areas. A daily service runs from Tewkesbury, Gloucester and Cheltenham to London.

The office is at Thomas House, St Margaret's Road, Cheltenham. The fleet livery is white, blue and red applied in various styles, but there are several variations. Newer coaches are silver with yellow, orange and red stripes.

Swanbrook was operating stage services in the Gloucester and Cheltenham area well before deregulation came about. Although coaches are often used on these duties, some buses are owned for stage carriage and school services. D123EFH is one of two Plaxton Derwent 55-seat Bedfords bought in 1987 and is seen at The Cross in central Gloucester. Note the fleet aims to obtain sequential registration figures for its new vehicles. Colin Martin

TALLY HO!

Wellington and Partners (Tally Ho Coaches), Industrial Estate, Kingsbridge, Devon, TQ7 1ES

W.S.O.Wellington started business in the 1930s with one or two coaches on private hire work. After the war a new partnership, William Wellington & Son, carried on the business from Belle Vue Road, Kingsbridge. At East Allington, near Totnes, J.H.Clarke commenced in almost the same way before the Second World War, but afterwards he expanded a little quicker and by 1951 was operating seventeen coaches under the fleetname Tally Ho!.

The Clarke and Wellington firms came together, trading as Tally Ho! Coaches at East Allington and a limited company Tally Ho! Coaches Ltd was formed in March 1960. Hoare of Ivybridge was taken over in June 1975 and in 1979 Sunshine Coaches of Plymouth was acquired. A new company Wellington and Partners (Tally Ho Coaches) was formed in 1984.

A large number of schools and works contract services are now operated in addition to British and Continental tours. Service 606, from Kingsbridge to Salcombe, is the most frequent of the four stage routes operated; others are market day services from Lee Mill to Mothecombe, Lee Mill to Ivybridge and Totnes to both Ermington and Berry Pomeroy. In January 1993 a new service commenced from Dartmouth with destinations including Exeter and Plymouth. This is operated on behalf of Devon County Council.

Fleet livery is white and blue. The garage is at Kingsbridge.

The Tally Ho! stage carriage fleet is largely based on Bristol chassis, of three distinct models. One of several former London Transport semi-automatic LH6Ls with 7ft 6in wide ECW bodies is KJD413P. It is seen in Kingsbridge. Barry Spencer

TRURONIAN

Truronian Ltd, 24 Lemon Street, Truro, Cornwall TF1 2LS

In September 1987 three members of the Western National management team, who had resigned after their own bid for Western National Ltd was rejected, purchased Truronian Tours from H.Brown who had run it for 25 years before retiring. In January 1988 the operation was expanded by the purchase of Flora Motors of Helston. Flora had operated stage services in the Lizard peninsula.

Stage service operation was extended when, in February 1988, Roseland Motors' Veryan to Truro service was taken over and, with a grant from the Rural Development Commission, services radiating from Helston was expanded. Current services include several routes gained in the Cornwall County Council tendering round in September 1991 and in addition to several routes in the area, operate the Truro City services, as well as less frequent stage and schools services. Private hire and excursions together with a full holiday programme are also undertaken. The Flora fleetname was perpetuated for a time but all vehicles are now in a livery of silver with red bands and stripes. Garages are at Newham Industrial Site, Truro and Clodgog Lane, Helston.

A particularly interesting vehicle in the Truronian fleet is this Leyland Atlantean 33-footer. It was built around 1970 and received an Alexander body tacked on to a Merseyside PTE order of special styling with long windows, etc. The vehicle then returned to Leyland for use as a test rig, until sold in 1980 to Rennie of Dunfermline, with whom it received the registration SFS159V. Even now it is known as the Flying Testbed, although the Austin Mini grille is not thought to be related to any of Leyland's development work! Roy Marshall

WAKE'S

Wake's Services (Sparkford) Ltd, Southgate Road, Wincanton, Somerset, BA9 9EB

Reginald Wake commenced operations in 1930 at South Barrow near Sparkford, with a fourteen-seat model T Ford and a Chevrolet coach. The bus was used on routes to Glastonbury, Shepton Mallet and Yeovil. Business gradually expanded with private hire and contracts, and with the extra work taken on during the war considerable expansion took place. Wakes provide an extensive excursions and tours programme from Wincanton, Yeovil, Gillingham and Sparkford.

The large amount of stage carriage work that was operated up to the 1960s and 1970s, which incidentally required the use of double-deck buses, went into decline and has left Wakes with two regular daily services; Service 1 from Shepton Mallet to Yeovil and Service 20 from Castle Cary to Wincanton, the latter supported by Somerset County. In addition, some twelve less-frequent commercial services, seven other tendered services for Somerset County Council, one tendered service for Dorset County Council and the Wincanton to Shaftesbury service are supported by Wiltshire County Council. Wakes vehicles now go as far as Minehead, Sturminster Newton, Shaftesbury, Salisbury, Glastonbury, Taunton and Dorchester.

Fleet livery is cream with pale blue trim and gold lettering. The head office and workshop are at Southgate Road, Wincanton with an outstation at Northfield Garage, Sparkford.

WILLIAMS

C R Williams (Coaches) Ltd, Trelyn, Goonbell, St Agnes, Cornwall, TR5 0PW

C.R.Williams started stage services in February 1970 and currently uses double-deck buses on the six-journey per day service 287 from St Agnes to Truro operated on behalf of Cornwall County Council. Wednesday service 284 is also operated, linking Truro with Trevellas.

Vehicles are based in St Agnes.

Williams of St Agnes run a commercial service from St Agnes, on the north Cornwall coast, direct across to Truro, on an inlet of the south Cornwall coast. It runs via Threemilestone, six times a day. In their small fleet is this late-model Bedford, a YNV with the oddly-proportioned Plaxton Supreme VI coachwork, supplied new as NCV942X in 1982.
Roy Marshall

GUERNSEYBUS

Guernseybus Ltd, Picquet House, St Peter Port, Guernsey.

Public transport originated on the island in 1837 when horse buses were introduced between St Peter Port and St Sampsons. Steam trams commenced in 1879 with electric trams operating between 1891 and 1934. The company commenced trading on 16th February 1981 with vehicles and facilities of the Guernsey Railway Company. The latter had ceased trading suddenly during December 1980 with no bus operation in the intervening period.

Since 1981, the former Railway Company Albions have all been replaced, as have most of the Bedfords. The replacements were initially Bristol SULs though a large number of Bristol LHs are now operated. A general width restriction of 7ft 4in, with only certain roads relaxed to 7ft 6in, has influenced purchases. Only vehicles with an 'A' prefix to the fleet number are allowed on all roads.

Index marks on Guernsey consist entirely of numbers, but re-registrations occasionally take place within the fleet. Fleet livery is white although a large proportion of the fleet carry all-over advertisements, frequently retaining the white base colour. Workshops and garage are at Grand Bouet, St Peter Port.

Pictured at Pleinmont is Guernseybus 53, a Bristol LH which spent most of its life with London Buses on a Hillingdon sponsored service. Keith Grimes

JERSEY

Jersey Motor Transport Co Ltd, 2-4 Caledonia Place, St Helier, Jersey.

Public transport on the Channel Island of Jersey started with a horsebus route from St Helier to St Aubin in the late 18th century. Motorbus operation commenced briefly in 1910 and again in 1918 causing the railway to introduce feeder services to halt passenger decline. The railway closed in 1937. Gradually, the numerous operators have merged until by 1978 there was only one operator of stage services, JMB.

Rapid modernisation of the fleet has taken place since the 1960s, initially using the Ford chassis. Fleet livery is blue and white, though many carry overall advertisements. The fleet is maintained in Caledonia Place, St Helier, with the adjacent bus station being used for additional parking. New deliveries normally take the lowest available fleet number with registrations consisting of numbers prefixed with the letter J.

This Willowbrook bodied Ford dates from 1975 and carries Jersey Motor Bus's standard livery of blue and white. Most buses on the island carry all-over adverts. Keith Grimes

BADGERLINE

100-113
Volvo B10M-61 — Alexander P — DP53F — 1987

100	D100GHY	103	D103GHY	106	D106GHY	109	D109GHY	112	D112GHY
101	D101GHY	104	D104GHY	107	D107GHY	110	D110GHY	113	D113GHY
102	D102GHY	105	D105GHY	108	D108GHY	111	D111GHY		

1257-1332
Bristol RELL6L — Eastern Coach Works — B50F — 1972/73 Ex Bristol, 1986

1257	DAE511K	1297	EHU391K	1316	LHT170L	1317	LHT171L	1332	OAE954M
1292	EHU386K	1302	HHW915L						

2071	GHY133K	Bristol RELH6L	Eastern Coach Works	DP49F	1972 Ex Bristol, 1986
2098	VJT738	Leyland Leopard PSU3E/4R	Plaxton P'mount 3200(1983) C49F	1977	Ex Bristol, 1986
2110	816SHW	Leyland Leopard PSU5D/4R	Plaxton Supreme V	C50F	1980 Ex Wallace Arnold, 1986

2203-2210
Leyland Tiger TRCTL11/3R — Plaxton Paramount 3200 — C53F* — 1983 — *2203/4 are C57F

2203	A203RHT	2205	530OHU	2207	CSV303	2209	CSV992	2210	A210SAE
2204	A204RHT	2206	CSV231	2208	CSV524				

2221	B221WEU	Leyland Tiger TRCTL11/3R	Duple Laser 2	C47FT	1984 Ex Bristol, 1986
2222	B222WEU	Leyland Tiger TRCTL11/3R	Duple Laser 2	C47FT	1984 Ex Bristol, 1986
2223	VCL461	Leyland Tiger TRCTL11/3R	Duple Laser 2	C47FT	1984 Ex Bristol, 1986

2500-2507
Volvo B10M-61 — Van Hool Alizée H — C48FT* — 1987 — *2500-3 are C53F

2500	D500GHY	2502	D502GHY	2504	D504GHY	2506	D506GHY	2507	D507GHY
2501	D501GHY	2503	D503GHY	2505	D505GHY				

2510	D510HHW	Volvo B10M-61	Van Hool Alizée H	C48FT	1987 Ex Western National, 1992
2600	D600GHY	Volvo B10M-61	Van Hool Alizée	C57F	1987
2601	D601GHY	Volvo B10M-61	Van Hool Alizée	C57F	1987

3017-3027
Leyland National 11351/1R — B52F — 1975-76 Ex Bristol, 1986

3017	JHW105P	3019	KHT117P	3023	KHT121P	3025	KHT123P	3027	KHT125P
3018	KHT116P								

3028-3080
Leyland National 11351A/1R — B52F — 1976-79 Ex Bristol, 1986

3028	NFB596R	3036	NFB604R	3041	OHW492R	3067	TTC535T	3072	TTC540T
3029	NFB597R	3037	NFB605R	3042	OHW493R	3068	TTC536T	3078	YFB969V
3031	NFB599R	3038	OHW489R	3054	SAE757S	3069	TTC537T	3079	YFB970V
3032	NFB600R	3039	OHW490R	3055	SAE758S	3070	TTC538T	3080	YFB971V
3033	NFB601R	3040	OHW491R	3065	TTC533T	3071	TTC539T		

3501-3534
Leyland National 2 NL116L11/1R — B52F* — 1980 — Ex Bristol, 1986
*3518-20 are DP47F, 3525 is DP48F, 3532/3 are DP49F, 3517 is DP52F.

3501	AAE645V	3511	AAE655V	3518	AAE662V	3526	BOU1V	3530	BOU5V
3508	AAE652V	3512	AAE656V	3519	AAE663V	3527	BOU2V	3532	BOU7V
3509	AAE653V	3513	AAE657V	3520	AAE664V	3528	BOU3V	3533	BOU8V
3510	AAE654V	3517	AAE661V	3525	BHY999V	3529	BOU4V	3534	DHW349W

3535	BVP819V	Leyland National 2 NL116L11/1R	B49F	1980	Ex Midland Red West, 1989
3536	BVP820V	Leyland National 2 NL116L11/1R	B49F	1980	Ex Midland Red West, 1989

3601-3605
Leyland National 2 NL116HLXCT/1R — DP47F — 1984 — Ex Midland Red West, 1989

3601	A201YWP	3602	A202YWP	3603	A203YWP	3604	A204YWP	3605	A205YWP

3610-3616
Leyland Lynx LX2R11C15Z4R — Leyland — B49F — 1990

3610	H610YTC	3612	H612YTC	3614	H614YTC	3615	H615YTC	3616	H616YTC
3611	H611YTC	3613	H613YTC						

3800-3823 Mercedes-Benz 811D Optare StarRider B31F* 1988 *3810 is B33F
3819/21-3 are DP27F

3800	E800MOU	3804	E804MOU	3810	E810MOU	3815	E815MOU	3819	E819MOU
3801	E801MOU	3805	E805MOU	3811	E811MOU	3816	E816MOU	3821	E821MOU
3802	E802MOU	3806	E806MOU	3813	E813MOU	3817	E817MOU	3822	E822MOU
3803	E803MOU	3809	E809MOU	3814	E814MOU	3818	E818MOU	3823	E823MOU

3850-3866 Mercedes-Benz 709D Reeve Burgess Beaver B23F 1991-92

3850	J850FTC	3854	J854FTC	3858	J858FTC	3861	J861HWS	3864	J864HWS
3851	J851FTC	3855	J855FTC	3859	J859FTC	3862	J862HWS	3865	J865HWS
3852	J852FTC	3856	J856FTC	3860	J860HWS	3863	J863HWS	3866	J866HWS
3853	J853FTC	3857	J857FTC						

4436-4459 Ford Transit 190 Dormobile B16F 1985 Ex Bristol, 1986

4436	B436WTC	4443	B443WTC	4449	B449WTC	4453	B454WTC	4457	B457WTC
4437	B437WTC	4446	B446WTC	4450	B450WTC	4455	B455WTC	4458	B458WTC
4439	B439WTC	4448	B448WTC	4452	B452WTC	4456	B456WTC	4459	B459WTC

4474	B474WTC	Ford Transit 190	Carlyle	DP16F	1985	Ex Bristol, 1986
4475	B475YEU	Ford Transit 190	Carlyle	DP16F	1985	Ex Bristol, 1986

4480-4531 Ford Transit 190 Dormobile B16F 1985-86
4487-94/502-13/7-20/2-9/31 ex Bristol, 1986

4480	C480BFB	4499	C499BFB	4514	C514BFB	4521	C521BFB	4527	C527BFB
4481	C481BFB	4500	C500BFB	4515	C515BFB	4522	C522BFB	4529	C529BFB
4487	C487BFB	4502	C502BFB	4516	C516BFB	4523	C523BFB	4530	C530BFB
4493	C493BFB	4512	C512BFB	4517	C517BFB	4525	C525BFB	4531	C531BFB
4494	C494BFB	4513	C513BFB	4520	C520BFB	4526	C525BFB		

4532-4567 Ford Transit 190 Dormobile B16F* 1986 *4548-50 are DP16F

4532	C532BHY	4539	C539BHY	4546	C546BHY	4554	C554BHY	4561	C561BHY
4533	C533BHY	4540	C540BHY	4547	C547BHY	4555	C555BHY	4562	C562BHY
4534	C534BHY	4541	C541BHY	4548	C548BHY	4556	C556BHY	4563	C563BHY
4535	C535BHY	4542	C542BHY	4549	C549BHY	4557	C557BHY	4564	C564BHY
4536	C536BHY	4543	C543BHY	4550	C550BHY	4558	C558BHY	4565	C565BHY
4537	C537BHY	4544	C544BHY	4551	C551BHY	4559	C559BHY	4566	C566BHY
4538	C538BHY	4545	C545BHY	4552	C552BHY	4560	C560BHY	4567	C567BHY

4589-4600 Ford Transit VE6 Dormobile B16F 1986 Ex Western National, 1987

4589	D72KRL	4592	D75KRL	4594	D77KRL	4596	D79KRL	4598	D81KRL
4590	D73KRL	4593	D76KRL	4595	D78KRL	4597	D80KRL	4600	D83KRL
4591	D74KRL								

4900-4943 Iveco Daily 49.10 Robin Hood B19F* 1986-87 4928 ex Midland Red West, 1990
*4907/43 are DP19F

4900	D900GEU	4905	D905HOU	4928	E928KEU	4936	E936KEU	4940	E940KEU
4901	D901GEU	4906	D906HOU	4932	E932KEU	4937	E937KEU	4941	E941KEU
4902	D902HOU	4907	D907HOU	4933	E933KEU	4938	E938KEU	4942	E942KEU
4903	D903HOU	4909	D909HOU	4934	E934KEU	4939	E939KEU	4943	E943LAE
4904	D904HOU	4926	E926KEU	4935	E935KEU				

4950	E209BOD	Iveco Daily 49.10	Reeve Burgess Beaver	B21F	1988	Ex Western National, 1992
4951	E210BOD	Iveco Daily 49.10	Reeve Burgess Beaver	B21F	1988	Ex Western National, 1992
4952	E211BOD	Iveco Daily 49.10	Reeve Burgess Beaver	B21F	1988	Ex Western National, 1992
4953	E212BOD	Iveco Daily 49.10	Reeve Burgess Beaver	B21F	1988	Ex Western National, 1992
5000	C28EUH	Leyland Olympian ONTL11/2R	East Lancashire	CH47/31F	1985	Ex G&G, Leamington, 1989
5001	C29EUH	Leyland Olympian ONTL11/2R	East Lancashire	CH47/31F	1985	Ex G&G, Leamington, 1989
5146	AHU523V	Bristol VRT/SL3/6LXB	Eastern Coach Works	DPH39/28F	1980	Ex Bristol, 1986
5501	HTC727N	Bristol VRT/SL2/6LXB	Eastern Coach Works	H39/31F	1975	Ex Bristol, 1986
5505	KOU791P	Bristol VRT/SL3/6LXB	Eastern Coach Works	H39/31F	1976	Ex Bristol, 1986
5506	KOU792P	Bristol VRT/SL3/6LXB	Eastern Coach Works	H39/31F	1976	Ex Bristol, 1986
5508	KOU794P	Bristol VRT/SL3/6LXB	Eastern Coach Works	H39/31F	1976	Ex Bristol, 1986
5509	KOU795P	Bristol VRT/SL3/6LXB	Eastern Coach Works	H39/31F	1976	Ex Bristol, 1986
5511	LHT721P	Bristol VRT/SL3/501(6LXB)	Eastern Coach Works	H39/31F	1976	Ex Bristol, 1986

5516-5526 Bristol VRT/SL3/6LXB   Eastern Coach Works   DPH43/31F* 1977-78 Ex Bristol, 1986
                                                                  *5516/23 is H43/31F

| 5516 | PEU511R | 5518 | PEU513R | 5522 | PEU517R | 5523 | PEU518R | 5526 | RFB616S |
| 5517 | PEU512R | 5519 | PEU514R | | | | | | |

5529-5546 Bristol VRT/SL3/680   Eastern Coach Works   H43/31F* 1981 Ex Bristol, 1986
                                                                  *5529/33/4/7/44 now 6LXB; 5529/37/44 are DPH43/31F

5529	DHW351W	5534	EWS742W	5537	EWS745W	5542	EWS750W	5545	EWS753W
5531	EWS739W	5536	EWS744W	5541	EWS749W	5544	EWS752W	5546	EWS754W
5533	EWS741W								

5550	STW26W	Bristol VRT/SL3/6LXB	Eastern Coach Works	H39/31F	1980	Ex Thamesway, 1991
5551	KOO792V	Bristol VRT/SL3/6LXB	Eastern Coach Works	H39/31F	1980	Ex Thamesway, 1991
5552	UVX2S	Bristol VRT/SL3/501(6LXB)	Eastern Coach Works	H39/31F	1977	Ex Thamesway, 1991
5553	KOO791V	Bristol VRT/SL3/6LXB	Eastern Coach Works	H39/31F	1980	Ex Thamesway, 1991
5554	KOO793V	Bristol VRT/SL3/6LXB	Eastern Coach Works	H39/31F	1980	Ex Thamesway, 1991
5555	LBD922V	Bristol VRT/SL3/6LXB	Eastern Coach Works	H43/31F	1979	Ex Thamesway, 1991
5556	FRP906T	Bristol VRT/SL3/6LXB	Eastern Coach Works	H43/31F	1978	Ex Thamesway, 1991
5557	STW29W	Bristol VRT/SL3/6LXB	Eastern Coach Works	H39/31F	1980	Ex Western National, 1992
5558	STW31W	Bristol VRT/SL3/6LXC(6LXB)	Eastern Coach Works	H39/31F	1980	Ex Thamesway, 1992
5559	STW32W	Bristol VRT/SL3/6LXB	Eastern Coach Works	H39/31F	1980	Ex Thamesway, 1992
5560	STW33W	Bristol VRT/SL3/6LXB	Eastern Coach Works	H39/31F	1980	Ex Thamesway, 1992
5561	STW34W	Bristol VRT/SL3/6LXB	Eastern Coach Works	H39/31F	1980	Ex Thamesway, 1992
5562	XHK221X	Bristol VRT/SL3/6LXB	Eastern Coach Works	H43/31F	1981	Ex Thamesway, 1992
5563	XHK222X	Bristol VRT/SL3/6LXB	Eastern Coach Works	H43/31F	1981	Ex Thamesway, 1992
5564	XHK224X	Bristol VRT/SL3/6LXB	Eastern Coach Works	H43/31F	1981	Ex Thamesway, 1992
5565	XHK227X	Bristol VRT/SL3/6LXB	Eastern Coach Works	H43/31F	1981	Ex Thamesway, 1992
5600	JNU136N	Bristol VRT/SL2/6LX	Eastern Coach Works	H39/31F	1975	Ex Bristol, 1986
5615	MUA874P	Bristol VRT/SL3/6LX	Eastern Coach Works	H43/31F	1975	Ex Bristol, 1986

5700-5711 Volvo Citybus B10M-50   Alexander RH   DPH47/35F 1987

5700	D700GHY	5703	D703GHY	5706	D706GHY	5708	D708GHY	5710	D710GHY
5701	D701GHY	5704	D704GHY	5707	D707GHY	5709	D709GHY	5711	D711GHY
5702	D702GHY	5705	D705GHY						

5712	E215BTA	Volvo Citybus B10M-50	Alexander RH	DPH47/35F	1988	Ex Western National, 1989
5713	E216BTA	Volvo Citybus B10M-50	Alexander RH	DPH47/35F	1988	Ex Western National, 1989
5714	E217BTA	Volvo Citybus B10M-50	Alexander RH	DPH47/35F	1988	Ex Western National, 1989

6000-6004 MCW Metrobus DR103/4   MCW   DPH43/30F* 1980 Ex Bristol, 1986
                                                           *6000 is DPH43/29F

| 6000 | DAE510W | 6001 | DAE511W | 6002 | DAE512W | 6003 | DAE513W | 6004 | DAE514W |

8583	GHT127	Bristol K5G	Eastern Coach Works	O33/26R	1941	Ex Bristol, 1990
8600	RTH931S	Bristol VRT/SL3/501	Eastern Coach Works	CO43/31F	1977	Ex South Wales, 1991
8601	RTH932S	Bristol VRT/SL3/501	Eastern Coach Works	CO43/31F	1977	Ex South Wales, 1991
8604	612UKM	Leyland Atlantean PDR1/1 MK2	Weymann	O44/33F	1963	Ex Bristol, 1986
8606	VDV137S	Bristol VRT/SL3/6LXB	Eastern Coach Works	CO43/31F	1977	Ex Western National, 1990
8608	UFX860S	Bristol VRT/SL3/6LXB	Eastern Coach Works	CO43/31F	1977	Ex Bristol, 1986

8609-8614 Leyland Olympian ONLXB/1R   Roe   CO47/29F 1984 Ex Bristol, 1986

| 8609 | A809THW | 8611 | A811THW | 8612 | A812THW | 8613 | A813THW | 8614 | A814THW |
| 8610 | A810THW | | | | | | | | |

8615-8619 Bristol VRT/SL3/6LXB   Eastern Coach Works   O43/29F 1975-76 Ex Bristol, 1986

| 8615 | JHW107P | 8616 | JHW108P | 8617 | JHW109P | 8618 | JHW112P | 8619 | JHW114P |

| 8620 | LEU256P | Bristol VRT/SL3/6LXB | Eastern Coach Works | O43/27D | 1976 | Ex Bristol, 1989 |
| 8621 | LEU269P | Bristol VRT/SL3/6LXB | Eastern Coach Works | O43/27D | 1976 | Ex Bristol, 1990 |

9001-9010 Leyland Olympian ONCL10/1RZ Leyland   H47/31F* 1989 *9009/10 are DPH43/29F

| 9001 | G901TWS | 9003 | G903TWS | 9005 | G905TWS | 9007 | G907TWS | 9009 | G909TWS |
| 9002 | G902TWS | 9004 | G904TWS | 9006 | G906TWS | 9008 | G908TWS | 9010 | G910TWS |

9506-9532 Leyland Olympian ONLXB/1R Roe DPH43/29F* 1982-83 Ex Bristol, 1986
*9514 is DPH43/25F

9506	JHU905X	9509	JHU908X	9511	JHU910X	9514	JHU913X	9531	NTC130Y
9507	JHU906X	9510	JHU909X	9512	JHU911X	9516	LWS32Y	9532	NTC131Y
9508	JHU907X								

Previous Registrations:

530OHU	A205SAE	CSV303	A207SAE	VCL461	B223WEU
816SHW	LUA284V	CSV524	A208SAE	VJT738	PWS492S
CSV231	A206SAE	CSV992	A209SAE		

Special Liveries:
1972 livery: 1257
Bath Opentop service: 8583, 8600/1/6/8/15-7/20/1
Overall Advertisements: 3801, 5555, 9007, 9507
National Express/Rapide: 2221, 2500-7/10.

Named Vehicles:
8583 *Prince Bladud*, 8600 *I.K.Brunel*, 8601 *William Herschel*, 8606 *Minerva*, 8608 *John Wood*, 8615 *Sally Lunn*, 8616 *Beau Nash*, 8617 *Ralph Allen*, 8620 *King Edgar*, 8621 *Dr William Oliver*.

CHELTENHAM & GLOUCESTER / SWINDON & DISTRICT

101-105 Leyland Olympian ONLXB/2RZ Alexander RL H51/36F 1990

101	G101AAD	102	G102AAD	103	G103AAD	104	G104AAD	105	G105AAD

106-111 Leyland Titan TNLXB/1RF Park Royal H47/26F 1979-80 Ex Thames Transit, 1990

106	GNF6V	108	GNF8V	109	GNF9V	110	GNF10V	111	GNF11V

301-313 Leyland National 11351A/1R(DAF) B52F* 1977-79 Ex Bristol, 1983
*301 is B25DL/B52F

301	TAE645S	304	PHW985S	307	SAE752S	310	VEU231T	312	TAE644S
302	YFB973V	305	PHW989S	308	TAE642S	311	SAE756S	313	TAE639S
303	TAE641S	306	PHW988S	309	SAE754S				

600	A871KDF	Mercedes-Benz L608D	PMT	DP18F	1984	
605	B447WTC	Ford Transit 190	Dormobile	B16F	1985	Ex Badgerline, 1992
606	B470WTC	Ford Transit 190	Carlyle	B16F	1985	Ex Badgerline, 1992
607	C705FKE	Ford Transit 190	Dormobile	B16F	1986	Ex East Kent, 1991
608	C715FKE	Ford Transit 190	Dormobile	B16F	1986	Ex East Kent, 1991
609	C716FKE	Ford Transit 190	Dormobile	B16F	1986	Ex East Kent, 1991
610	C724FKE	Ford Transit 190	Dormobile	B16F	1986	Ex East Kent, 1991
611	B205GNL	Ford Transit 190	Alexander AM	DP16F	1985	Ex Go-Ahead, 1990
612	B206GNL	Ford Transit 190	Alexander AM	B16F	1985	Ex Go-Ahead, 1990
613	C723FKE	Ford Transit 190	Dormobile	B16F	1986	Ex East Kent, 1990

614-645 Ford Transit 190 Alexander AM B16F* 1985 *644 is DP16F

614	C614SFH	626	C626SFH	632	C632SFH	637	C637SFH	642	C642SFH
615	C615SFH	627	C627SFH	633	C633SFH	638	C638SFH	643	C643SFH
617	C617SFH	629	C629SFH	634	C634SFH	639	C639SFH	644	C644SFH
618	C618SFH	630	C630SFH	635	C635SFH	640	C640SFH	645	C645SFH
621	C621SFH	631	C631SFH	636	C636SFH	641	C641SFH		

649-662 Mercedes-Benz L608D Alexander AM B20F 1986

649	C649XDF	652	C652XDF	655	C655XDF	658	C658XDF	661	C661XDF
650	C650XDF	653	C653XDF	656	C656XDF	659	C659XDF	662	C662XDF
651	C651XDF	654	C654XDF	657	C657XDF	660	C660XDF		

663-676 MCW MetroRider MF150 MCW B25F* 1987-88 *670/1/5/6 are DP25F

663	E663JAD	666	E666JAD	669	E669JAD	672	E672KDG	675	E675KDG
664	E664JAD	667	E667JAD	670	E670JDG	673	E673KDG	676	E676KDG
665	E665JAD	668	E668JAD	671	E671JDG	674	E674KDG		

677	F677PDF	Mercedes-Benz 709D	PMT	B25F	1988	
678	F311DET	Mercedes-Benz 709D	Reeve Burgess Beaver	B25F	1988	Ex Reeve Burgess, 1989

679-684   Mercedes-Benz 709D   PMT   B25F   1989

679	G679AAD	681	G681AAD	682	G682AAD	683	G683AAD	684	G684AAD
680	G680AAD								

700-714   Leyland National 10351B/1R   B44F   1978-79 Ex Bristol, 1983

700	VAE499T	703	VAE502T	708	VAE507T	713	XEU861T	714	YEU446V
702	VAE501T	707	VAE506T						

801	K801TDF	Mercedes-Benz 811D	Wright Handybus	B33F	1993	
802	K802TDF	Mercedes-Benz 811D	Wright Handybus	B33F	1993	
2200	A200RHT	Leyland Tiger TRCTL11/3R	Plaxton Paramount 3200 E	C57F	1983	Ex Bristol, 1983
2202	A202RHT	Leyland Tiger TRCTL11/3R	Plaxton Paramount 3200 E	C57F	1983	Ex Bristol, 1983
2211	A211SAE	Leyland Tiger TRCTL11/3R	Plaxton Paramount 3200 E	C53F	1983	
2212	A212SAE	Leyland Tiger TRCTL11/3R	Plaxton Paramount 3200 E	C49FT	1983	
2213	A213SAE	Leyland Tiger TRCTL11/3R	Plaxton Paramount 3200 E	C53F	1983	
2214	A214SAE	Leyland Tiger TRCTL11/3R	Plaxton Paramount 3200 E	C53F	1983	
2215	511OHU	Leyland Tiger TRCTL11/3RH	Plaxton Paramount 3500 II	C46FT	1985	
2216	HIL6075	Leyland Tiger TRCTL11/3RH	Plaxton Paramount 3500 II	C49FT	1985	
2217	A873MRW	Leyland Tiger TRCTL11/3R	Plaxton Paramount 3200	C51F	1984	Ex Midland Red South, 1990
2224	498FYB	Leyland Tiger TRCTL11/3R	Plaxton Paramount 3200	C50F	1983	Ex Black & White, 1985
2403	467WYA	Leyland Tiger TRCTL11/3R	Plaxton Paramount 3200	C50F	1983	Ex Black & White, 1985
2406	YJV806	Leyland Royal Tiger B50	Roe Doyen	C50F	1983	Ex Black & White, 1985
2408	C422WFH	Leyland Tiger TRCTL11/3RZ	Plaxton Paramount 3500 II	C46FT	1986	
2409	C423WFH	Leyland Tiger TRCTL11/3RZ	Plaxton Paramount 3500 II	C46FT	1986	
2410	C424WFH	Leyland Tiger TRCTL11/3RZ	Plaxton Paramount 3500 II	C46FT	1986	

3006-3010   Leyland National 11351/1R   B49F   1975 Ex Midland Red South, 1992

3006	GOL406N	3007	GOL407N	3008	GOL408N	3009	GOL409N	3010	GOL410N

3011	HEU120N	Leyland National 11351/1R	B52F	1975	Ex Badgerline, 1991
3012	GOL413N	Leyland National 11351/1R	B49F	1975	Ex Midland Red South, 1992
3013	HEU122N	Leyland National 11351/1R	B52F	1975	Ex Bristol, 1983
3014	GOL426N	Leyland National 11351/1R	B49F	1975	Ex Midland Red South, 1991
3015	JHW103P	Leyland National 11351/1R	B52F	1975	Ex Bristol, 1983
3024	KHT122P	Leyland National 11351/1R	B52F	1976	Ex Bristol, 1983
3026	KHT124P	Leyland National 11351/1R	B52F	1976	Ex Bristol, 1983
3034	NFB602R	Leyland National 11351A/1R	B52F	1976	Ex Bristol, 1983
3035	NFB603R	Leyland National 11351A/1R	B52F	1976	Ex Bristol, 1983

3036-3042   Leyland National 11351A/1R   B49F   1976-77 Ex Midland Red South, 1991-92

3036	NOE569R	3038	NOE584R	3040	NOE587R	3041	NOE555R	3042	NOE554R
3037	NOE551R	3039	NOE585R						

3044-3081   Leyland National 11351A/1R   B52F   1977-79 Ex Bristol, 1983

3044	PHW986S	3050	SAE753S	3058	UHW101T	3073	VEU228T	3077	VEU232T
3045	PHW987S	3052	SAE755S	3061	TAE643S	3074	VEU229T	3081	YFB972V
3048	SAE751S	3056	TAE638S	3064	TTC532T	3075	VEU230T		

3500-3531   Leyland National 2 NL116L11/1R   B52F   1980 Ex Bristol, 1983

3500	AAE644V	3504	AAE648V	3507	AAE651V	3516	AAE660V	3523	BHY997V
3502	AAE646V	3505	AAE649V	3514	AAE658V	3521	AAE665V	3524	BHY998V
3503	AAE647V	3506	AAE650V	3515	AAE659V	3522	BHY996V	3531	BOU6V

5030	JOU160P	Bristol VRT/SL3/501(6LXB)	Eastern Coach Works	H43/28F	1975	Ex Bristol, 1983

5065-5133   Bristol VRT/SL3/6LXB   Eastern Coach Works   H43/28F*   1976-79 Ex Bristol, 1983
*5089-93 are H43/27D

5065	MOU739R	5089	NHU672R	5092	NWS289R	5120	REU310S	5125	TWS906T
5087	NHU670R	5090	NWS287R	5093	NWS290R	5121	REU311S	5132	TWS913T
5088	NHU671R	5091	NWS288R	5119	REU309S	5122	TWS903T	5133	TWS914T

5512	LHT722P	Bristol VRT/SL3/501(6LXB)	Eastern Coach Works	H39/31F	1976	Ex Bristol, 1983
5514	LHT724P	Bristol VRT/SL3/501(6LXB)	Eastern Coach Works	H39/31F	1976	Ex Bristol, 1983

5515	LHT725P	Bristol VRT/SL3/501(6LXB)	Eastern Coach Works	H39/31F	1976	Ex Bristol, 1983
5520	PEU515R	Bristol VRT/SL3/6LXB	Eastern Coach Works	H43/31F	1977	Ex Bristol, 1983
5521	PEU516R	Bristol VRT/SL3/6LXB	Eastern Coach Works	H43/31F	1977	Ex Bristol, 1983
5527	RFB617S	Bristol VRT/SL3/6LXB	Eastern Coach Works	H43/31F	1978	Ex Bristol, 1983

5528-5543

	Bristol VRT/SL3/680*	Eastern Coach Works	H43/31F	1981	Ex Bristol, 1983 *5538 now Gardner

5528	DHW350W	5532	EWS740W	5538	EWS746W	5540	EWS748W	5543	EWS751W
5530	DHW352W	5535	EWS743W						

5613	MUA872P	Bristol VRT/SL3/6LX	Eastern Coach Works	H43/31F	1975	Ex Bristol, 1983

5619-5624

	Bristol VRT/SL3/6LXB	Eastern Coach Works	H43/31F*	1978	Ex Devon General, 1987 *5619 is H43/29F

5619	XDV602S	5621	VOD593S	5622	VOD596S	5623	VOD597S	5624	VOD598S
5620	XDV606S								

9500-9533

	Leyland Olympian ONLXB/1R	Roe		H47/29F	1982-83	Ex Bristol, 1983 9507 ex Yorkshire Rider, 1987

9500	JHU899X	9517	LWS33Y	9520	LWS36Y	9523	LWS39Y	9525	LWS41Y
9507	UWW7X	9518	LWS34Y	9521	LWS37Y	9524	LWS40Y	9533	NTC132Y
9513	JHU912X	9519	LWS35Y	9522	LWS38Y				

Operating Unit Liveries:

Cheltenham District: 301/4/6/11/2, 702/7, 2200-2410, 3008/10/3/5/24/61/4, 3500/4-7/24/31, 5030/87, 5620, 9519/21/33.

City of Gloucester: 302/3/5/7-10/3, 700/3/8/13/4, 3006/9/14/34/6/8-42/56/8, 5089-93, 5119/21/32/3, 5613/21, 9500/7/13/23-5.

Stroud Valleys: 600/15/77, 3011/2/35/7/44/5/8/50/2/73-5/7/81, 3502/3/14, 5065, 5528/30/2/5/8/40/3, 5619, 9517/8/20/2.

Metro: 605-12/4-76/80-4.

Swindon & District: 101-6/8-11, 801/2, 2217, 3007/26, 3515/6/21-3, 5088, 5120/2/5, 5512/4/5/20/7, 5622-4.

Previous Registrations:

467WYA	CDG206Y	511OHU	B215NDG	HIL6075	B216NDG
498FYB	CDG207Y	A873MRW	A71KDU, 552OHU	YJV806	DAD218Y

Special Liveries:

1929 Cheltenham District:	5030
All over white:	2200/13.
Black & White:	2202, 2403/6.
Cotswold:	678/9, 2211/4/24.
National Express:	2212/5/6, 2408-10
Overall Advertisements:	613, 9524.

CITY LINE

1460	OAE758R	Leyland National 11351A/2R		B49F	1977
1461	OAE759R	Leyland National 11351A/2R		B49F	1977

1600-1662

	Leyland Lynx LX2R11C15Z4R	Leyland	B49F	1989-90

1600	F600RTC	1613	F613RTC	1626	F626RTC	1639	H639YHT	1651	H651YHT
1601	F601RTC	1614	F614RTC	1627	F627RTC	1640	H640YHT	1652	H652YHT
1602	F602RTC	1615	F615RTC	1628	F628RTC	1641	H641YHT	1653	H653YHT
1603	F603RTC	1616	F616RTC	1629	F629RTC	1642	H642YHT	1654	H654YHT
1604	F604RTC	1617	F617RTC	1630	F630RTC	1643	H643YHT	1655	H655YHT
1605	F605RTC	1618	F618RTC	1631	F631RTC	1644	H644YHT	1656	H656YHT
1606	F606RTC	1619	F619RTC	1632	F632RTC	1645	H645YHT	1657	H657YHT
1607	F607RTC	1620	F620RTC	1633	H633YHT	1646	H646YHT	1658	H658YHT
1608	F608RTC	1621	F621RTC	1634	H634YHT	1647	H647YHT	1659	H659YHT
1609	F609RTC	1622	F622RTC	1636	H636YHT	1648	H648YHT	1660	H660YHT
1610	F610RTC	1623	F623RTC	1637	H637YHT	1649	H649YHT	1661	H661YHT
1611	F611RTC	1624	F624RTC	1638	H638YHT	1650	H650YHT	1662	H662YHT
1612	F612RTC	1625	F625RTC						

5055-5157 — Bristol VRT/SL3/6LXB — Eastern Coach Works — H43/27D* — 1976-80 *5055 is O43/27D

5055	LEU263P	5086	NFB122R	5110	RHY504S	5131	TWS912T	5145w	AHU522V
5070w	MOU744R	5096	NTC572R	5111	RHT505S	5134	TWS915T	5147w	AHW198V
5072w	MOU746R	5097	NTC573R	5112w	RHT506S	5135	AHU512V	5148w	AHW199V
5073	MOU747R	5098w	NTC574R	5113	RHT507S	5136w	AHU513V	5149w	AHW200V
5074w	MOU748R	5101w	PHY695S	5114w	RHT508S	5137	AHU514V	5150	AHW201V
5077w	NFB113R	5102w	PHY696S	5115w	RHT509S	5138	AHU515V	5151w	AHW202V
5078	NFB114R	5103	PHY697S	5116w	RHT510S	5139	AHU516V	5152	AHW203V
5079w	NFB115R	5105w	PHY699S	5117w	RHT511S	5140w	AHU517V	5153w	AHW204V
5080w	NFB116R	5106	PHY700S	5118	RHT512S	5141w	AHU518V	5154w	AHW205V
5082w	NFB118R	5107w	PHY701S	5127	TWS908T	5142w	AHU519V	5155	AHW206V
5084w	NFB120R	5108	PHY702S	5129	TWS910T	5143w	AHU520V	5156	AHW207V
5085	NFB121R	5109	RHY503S	5130	TWS911T	5144w	AHU521V	5157w	AHW208V

C7262	GAE883D	Bristol Lodekka FLF6G	Eastern Coach Works	H38/32F	1966	Ex Bristol, 1986

7468-7474 — Ford Transit 190D — Dormobile — B16F — 1986 — 7471/4 ex Brewers, 1992

7468	C468BHY	7470	C470BHY	7471	C471BHY	7473	C473BHY	7474	C474BHY
7469	C469BHY								

7476-7499 — Mercedes-Benz L608D — Reeve Burgess — B20F — 1986

7476	C476BHY	7482	C482BHY	7487	C487BHY	7492	C492BHY	7496	C496BHY
7477	C477BHY	7483	C483BHY	7488	C488BHY	7493	C493BHY	7497	C497BHY
7478	C478BHY	7484	C484BHY	7489	C489BHY	7494	C494BHY	7498	C498BHY
7480	C480BHY	7485	C485BHY	7490	C490BHY	7495	C495BHY	7499	C499BHY
7481	C481BHY	7486	C486BHY	7491	C491BHY				

7500-7569 — Mercedes-Benz L608D — Dormobile — B20F — 1986

7500	D500FAE	7514	D514FAE	7528	D528FAE	7542	D542FAE	7556	D556FAE
7501	D501FAE	7515	D515FAE	7529	D529FAE	7543	D543FAE	7557	D557FAE
7502	D502FAE	7516	D516FAE	7530	D530FAE	7544	D544FAE	7558	D558FAE
7503	D503FAE	7517	D517FAE	7531	D531FAE	7545	D545FAE	7559	D559FAE
7504	D504FAE	7518	D518FAE	7532	D532FAE	7546	D546FAE	7560	D560FAE
7505	D505FAE	7519	D519FAE	7533	D533FAE	7547	D547FAE	7561	D561FAE
7506	D506FAE	7520	D520FAE	7534	D534FAE	7548	D548FAE	7562	D562FAE
7507	D507FAE	7521	D521FAE	7535	D535FAE	7549	D549FAE	7563	D563FAE
7508	D508FAE	7522	D522FAE	7536	D536FAE	7550	D550FAE	7564	D564FAE
7509	D509FAE	7523	D523FAE	7537	D537FAE	7551	D551FAE	7565	D565FAE
7510	D510FAE	7524	D524FAE	7538	D538FAE	7552	D552FAE	7566	D566FAE
7511	D511FAE	7525	D525FAE	7539	D539FAE	7553	D553FAE	7567	D567FAE
7512	D512FAE	7526	D526FAE	7540	D540FAE	7554	D554FAE	7568	D568FAE
7513	D513FAE	7527	D527FAE	7541	D541FAE	7555	D555FAE	7569	D569FAE

7570-7617 — Iveco Daily 49.10 — Dormobile Routemaker — B20F — 1988-89

7570	E570NFB	7580	E580OOU	7590	F590OHT	7600	F600PWS	7609	F609PWS
7571	E571NFB	7581	E581OOU	7591	F591OHT	7601	F601PWS	7610	F610PWS
7572	E572NFB	7582	E582OOU	7592	F592OHT	7602	F602PWS	7611	F611PWS
7573	E573NFB	7583	E583OOU	7593	F593OHT	7603	F603PWS	7612	F612PWS
7574	E574NFB	7584	E584OOU	7594	F594OHT	7604	F604PWS	7613	F613PWS
7575	E575NFB	7585	E585OOU	7595	F595OHT	7605	F605PWS	7614	F614PWS
7576	E576NFB	7586	E586OOU	7596	F596OHT	7606	F606PWS	7615	F615PWS
7577	E577NFB	7587	E587OOU	7597	F597OHT	7607	F607PWS	7616	F616PWS
7578	F578OOU	7588	E588OOU	7598	F598PWS	7608	F608PWS	7617	F617PWS
7579	F579OOU	7589	E589OOU	7599	F599PWS				

7910-7921 — Iveco Daily 49.10 — Robin Hood — B19F — 1987 — Ex Badgerline, 1988

7910	D910HOU	7913	D913HOU	7916	D916HOU	7918	D918HOU	7920	D920HOU
7911	D911HOU	7914	D914HOU	7917	D917HOU	7919	D919HOU	7921	D921HOU
7912	D912HOU	7915	D915HOU						

7946-7958 — Iveco Daily 49.10 — Robin Hood — B19F — 1987 — Ex Red Admiral, 1989

7946	E946LAE	7949	E949LAE	7953	E953LAE	7955	E955LAE	7957	E957LAE
7947	E947LAE	7950	E950LAE	7954	E954LAE	7956	E956LAE	7958	E958LAE
7948	E948LAE								

| 8138 | D138NUS | Mercedes-Benz L608D | Alexander AM | B21F | 1986 | Ex Kelvin Central, 1992 |
| 8976 | E976MFB | Iveco Daily 49.10 | Dormobile Routemaker | B20F | 1988 | Ex Ford demonstrator, 1989 |

9501-9568

| | | Leyland Olympian ONLXB/1R | Roe | | H47/29F | 1982-84 |

9501	JHU900X	9530	NTC129Y	9541	NTC141Y	9551	A951SAE	9560	A960THW
9502	JHU901X	9534	NTC133Y	9543	NTC142Y	9552	A952SAE	9561	A961THW
9503	JHU902X	9535	NTC134Y	9544	NTC143Y	9553	A953SAE	9562	A962THW
9504	JHU903X	9536	NTC135Y	9545	A945SAE	9554	A954SAE	9563	A963THW
9505	JHU904X	9537	NTC136Y	9546	A946SAE	9555	A955THW	9564	A964THW
9515	JHU914X	9538	NTC137Y	9547	A947SAE	9556	A956THW	9565	A965THW
9526	LWS42Y	9539	NTC138Y	9548	A948SAE	9557	A957THW	9566	A966THW
9527	LWS43Y	9540	NTC139Y	9549	A949SAE	9558	A958THW	9567	A967THW
9528	LWS44Y	9541	NTC140Y	9550	A950SAE	9559	A959THW	9568	A968THW
9529	LWS45Y								

9601-9630

| | | Leyland Olympian ON2R56C16Z4 | Northern Counties Palatine | H44/32F | 1992-93 |

9601	K601LAE	9607	K607LAE	9613	K613LAE	9619	K619LAE	9625	K625LAE
9602	K602LAE	9608	K608LAE	9614	K614LAE	9620	K620LAE	9626	K626LAE
9603	K603LAE	9609	K609LAE	9615	K615LAE	9621	K621LAE	9627	K627LAE
9604	K604LAE	9610	K610LAE	9616	K616LAE	9622	K622LAE	9628	K628LAE
9605	K605LAE	9611	K611LAE	9617	K617LAE	9623	K623LAE	9629	K629LAE
9606	K606LAE	9612	K612LAE	9618	K618LAE	9624	K624LAE	9630	K630LAE

Special Liveries:
Guide Friday: 5055.
Overall Advertisements: 5109/11/34/55, 7913/5/7/21, 9539/44/55/61/6/7.

DEVON GENERAL EXETER / BAYLINE

7	A927MDV	Ford Transit 160	Carlyle	B16F	1985	
8	A928MDV	Ford Transit 160	PMT	B16F	1984	Ex Docklands Transit, 1992
9	A929MDV	Ford Transit 160	Carlyle	B16F	1984	Ex Blue Admiral, 1992
10	A930MDV	Ford Transit 160	Carlyle	B16F	1983	Ex Blue Admiral, 1992
11	A261MTA	Ford Transit 160	PMT	B16F	1984	Ex Docklands Transit, 1992
12	A262MTA	Ford Transit 160	Carlyle	B16F	1984	
13	A263MTA	Ford Transit 160	Carlyle	B16F	1984	
14	A264MTA	Ford Transit 160	PMT	B16F	1984	
15	A265MTA	Ford Transit 160	Carlyle	B16F	1984	
17	A687KDV	Ford Transit 160	Carlyle	B16F	1984	
18	A688KDV	Ford Transit 160	PMT	B16F	1984	

19-32

| | | Ford Transit 160 | Carlyle | B16F | 1984 |

19	A689KDV	22	A268MTA	26	A946MDV	29	A269MTA	31	A931MDV
20	A260MTA	23	A943MDV	27	A947MDV	30	A270MTA	32	A932MDV
21	A267MTA	25	A945MVD	28	A948MDV				

33	A933MDV	Ford Transit 160	Mellor	B16F	1984
35	A935MDV	Ford Transit 160	Mellor	B16F	1984
37	A937MDV	Ford Transit 160	Mellor	B16F	1984
38	A938MDV	Ford Transit 160	Carlyle	B16F	1984

39-46

| | | Ford Transit 160 | Mellor | B16F | 1984 |

39	A939MDV	41	A691KDV	42	A692KDV	43	A259MTA	46	B399UOD

48-93

| | | Mercedes-Benz 709D | Reeve Burgess Beaver | DP25F* | 1988 | *50/1 are B25F |

48	F748FDV	58	F718FDV	67	F727FDV	76	F736FDV	85	F745FDV
49	F749FDV	59	F719FDV	68	F728FDV	77	F737FDV	86	F756FDV
50	E829ATT	60	F720FDV	69	F729FDV	78	F738FDV	87	F757FDV
51	E830ATT	61	F721FDV	70	F730FDV	79	F739FDV	88	F758FDV
52	F712FDV	62	F722FDV	71	F731FDV	80	F740FDV	89	F759FDV
53	F713FDV	63	F723FDV	72	F732FDV	81	F741FDV	90	F760FDV
55	F715FDV	64	F724FDV	73	F733FDV	82	F742FDV	91	F761FDV
56	F716FDV	65	F725FDV	74	F734FDV	83	F743FDV	92	F762FDV
57	F717FDV	66	F726FDV	75	F735FDV	84	F744FDV	93	F763FDV

355-366

Mercedes-Benz 811D   Carlyle   B33F   1990

355	G831UDV	358	G834UDV	361	G837UDV	363	G839UDV	365	G841UDV
356	G832UDV	359	G835UDV	362	G838UDV	364	G840UDV	366	G842UDV
357	G833UDV	360	G836UDV						

480-496

Ford Transit 160   Robin Hood   B16F   1985-86

480	C480FFJ	484	C484FFJ	488	C480FFJ	491	C491FFJ	494	C494FFJ
481	C481FFJ	485	C485FFJ	489	C480FFJ	492	C492FFJ	495	C495FFJ
482	C482FFJ	486	C486FFJ	490	C490FFJ	493	C493FFJ	496	C496FFJ
483	C483FFJ	487	C487FFJ						

497-530

Ford Transit 160   Carlyle   B16F   1985-86

497	C497FFJ	504	C504FFJ	511	C511FFJ	518	C518FFJ	525	C525FFJ
498	C498FFJ	505	C505FFJ	512	C512FFJ	519	C519FFJ	526	C526FFJ
499	C499FFJ	506	C506FFJ	513	C513FFJ	520	C520FFJ	527	C527FFJ
500	C500FFJ	507	C507FFJ	514	C514FFJ	521	C521FFJ	528	C528FFJ
501	C501FFJ	508	C508FFJ	515	C515FFJ	522	C522FFJ	529	C529FFJ
502	C502FFJ	509	C509FFJ	516	C516FFJ	523	C523FFJ	530	C530FFJ
503	C503FFJ	510	C510FFJ	517	C517FFJ	524	C524FFJ		

535-551

Ford Transit 190   Carlyle   B16F   1985   Ex Thames Transit, 1989

535	C112DJO	539	C116DJO	543	C120DJO	546	C123DJO	549	C126DJO
536	C113DJO	540	C117DJO	544	C121DJO	547	C124DJO	550	C127DJO
537	C114DJO	541	C118DJO	545	C122DJO	548	C125DJO	551	C128DJO
538	C115DJO	542	C119DJO						

552-572

Ford Transit 190   Carlyle   B16F   1986   Ex Cityline, 1988-89

552	C402AHT	557	C407AHT	561	C411AHT	565	C415AHT	569	C419AHT
553	C403AHT	558	C408AHT	562	C412AHT	566	C416AHT	570	C420AHT
554	C404AHT	559	C409AHT	563	C413AHT	567	C417AHT	571	C421AHT
555	C405AHT	560	C410AHT	564	C414AHT	568	C418AHT	572	C422AHT
556	C406AHT								

588	C30BPR	Ford Transit 160	Carlyle	B16F	1986	Ex United Counties, 1988
589	C31BPR	Ford Transit 160	Carlyle	B16F	1986	Ex United Counties, 1988
590	C32BPR	Ford Transit 160	Carlyle	B16F	1986	Ex United Counties, 1988
591	C33BPR	Ford Transit 160	Carlyle	B16F	1986	Ex United Counties, 1988
592	D827UTF	Ford Transit 160	Carlyle	B16F	1986	Ex Hampshire Bus, 1988
593	D830UTF	Ford Transit 160	Carlyle	B16F	1986	Ex Hampshire Bus, 1988
594	D831UTF	Ford Transit 160	Carlyle	B16F	1986	Ex Hampshire Bus, 1988

657-699

Ford Transit 190   Carlyle   B16F   1986

657	C657FFJ	666	C666FFJ	675	C675FFJ	684	C684FFJ	692	C692FFJ
658	C658FFJ	667	C667FFJ	676	C676FFJ	685	C685FFJ	693	C693FFJ
659	C659FFJ	668w	C668FFJ	677	C677FFJ	686	C686FFJ	694	C694FFJ
660	C660FFJ	669	C669FFJ	678	C678FFJ	687	C687FFJ	695	C695FFJ
661	C661FFJ	670	C670FFJ	679	C679FFJ	688	C688FFJ	696	C696FFJ
662	C662FFJ	671	C671FFJ	680	C680FFJ	689	C689FFJ	697	C697FFJ
663	C663FFJ	672	C672FFJ	681	C681FFJ	690	C690FFJ	698	C698FFJ
664	C664FFJ	673	C673FFJ	682	C682FFJ	691	C691FFJ	699	C699FFJ
665	C665FFJ	674	C674FFJ	683	C683FFJ				

700-730

Ford Transit 190   Robin Hood   B16F   1986

700	C700FFJ	707	C707FFJ	713	C713FFJ	719	C719FFJ	725	C725FFJ
701	C701FFJ	708	C708FFJ	714	C714FFJ	720	C720FFJ	726	C726FFJ
702	C702FFJ	709	C709FFJ	715	C715FFJ	721	C721FFJ	727	C727FFJ
703	C703FFJ	710	C710FFJ	716	C716FFJ	722	C722FFJ	728	C728FFJ
704	C704FFJ	711	C711FFJ	717	C717FFJ	723	C723FFJ	729	C729FFJ
705	C705FFJ	712	C712FFJ	718	C718FFJ	724	C724FFJ	730	C730FFJ
706	C706FFJ								

731-767   Ford Transit 190   Carlyle   B16F   1986

731	C731FFJ	740	C740FFJ	747	C747FFJ	754	C754FFJ	761	C761FFJ
732	C732FFJ	741	C741FFJ	748	C748FFJ	755	C755FFJ	762	C762FFJ
733	C733FFJ	742	C742FFJ	749	C749FFJ	756	C756FFJ	763	C763FFJ
734	C734FFJ	743	C743FFJ	750	C750FFJ	757	C757FFJ	764	C764FFJ
735	C735FFJ	744	C744FFJ	751	C751FFJ	758	C758FFJ	765	C765FFJ
736	C736FFJ	745	C745FFJ	752	C752FFJ	759	C759FFJ	766	C766FFJ
737	C737FFJ	746	C746FFJ	753	C753FFJ	760	C760FFJ	767	C767FFJ
738	C738FFJ								

768	C227XRU	Ford Transit 190	Robin Hood	B18F	1985	Ex Hampshire Bus, 1986
769	D769NDV	Ford Transit 190	Carlyle	B16F	1986	
770	D770NDV	Ford Transit 190	Carlyle	B16F	1986	
935	VDV135S	Bristol VRT/SL3/6LXB	Eastern Coach Works	CO43/31F	1977	Ex Western National, 1983
954	H463GTM	Iveco Daily 49.10	Mellor	B19F	1991	

Named Vehicles: 7 *Little Willie*

Operations:

Bayline Ltd: 57/8, 64-8, 355-66, 480-6/8-509/11-26/8/37/8/4/5/7/52/6/8/60/2-5/7/9-72/88-90/2-4, 657-61/7-80/2/90/2/9, 732/69/70, 935.

Devon General: Remainder.

Special Liveries:

Exeter Bus Co (Blue/silver):	1/4/5, 531-3, 662, 705-31/4/6.	
Exeter Nipper (Green/gold):	487, 524/6/48/50/1, 666/91, 735/40-67.	
Exeter Minibus (Red/yellow):	7, 12-8, 22-34/6/8-41/6, 665, 704.	
Teignibus (Red/silver):	528, 700/32/69/70/5/7-700.	Matford Park & Ride: 663/4, 701-4.
Sowton Park & Ride:	42/3, 527, 737/8.	
Bayline (Ivory/maroon):	537/8/43/5/9/62/3/70/4/92-4,657-61/7-99.	
Brixham Coaches (Ivory/blue):	355-66.	Overall Advertisements: 480/95.

NORTH DEVON RED BUS / SOUTHERN NATIONAL

9	A33FVN	Leyland Tiger TRCTL11/3RZ	Plaxton Paramount 3500 III	C51F	1986	Ex Northumbria, 1987

50-54   Iveco Daily 49.10   Robin Hood   B21F   1987   Ex Southampton, 1990

50	D50ERV	51	D51ERV	52	D52ERV	53	D53ERV	54	D54ERV

91	GPD306N	Bristol LHS6L	Eastern Coach Works	B35F	1975	Ex Busways, 1990
92	GPD311N	Bristol LHS6L	Eastern Coach Works	B35F	1975	Ex Busways, 1990
93	OJD16R	Bristol LHS6L	Eastern Coach Works	B28F	1976	Ex Cummings, Blandford, 1989
94	FDV789V	Bristol LHS6L	Eastern Coach Works	B35F	1979	Ex Devon General, 1985
113	D113DRV	Iveco Daily 49.10	Robin Hood	B21F	1986	Ex People's Provincial, 1989
117	D117DRV	Iveco Daily 49.10	Robin Hood	B21F	1986	Ex People's Provincial, 1989
124	D124DRV	Iveco Daily 49.10	Robin Hood	B21F	1986	Ex People's Provincial, 1989
125	D125DRV	Iveco Daily 49.10	Robin Hood	B21F	1986	Ex People's Provincial, 1989

220-232   Iveco Daily 49.10   Robin Hood   B21F   1986   Ex Brighton & Hove, 1989

220	D220VCD	222	D222VCD	223	D223VCD	227	D227VCD	232	D232VCD
221	D221VCD								

280	DAD253T	Leyland Leopard PSU5C/4R	Plaxton Supreme IV	C57F	1979	Ex Black & White, 1985
281	DAD256T	Leyland Leopard PSU5C/4R	Plaxton Supreme IV	C57F	1979	Ex Black & White, 1985
282	DAD257T	Leyland Leopard PSU5C/4R	Plaxton Supreme IV	C57F	1979	Ex Black & White, 1985
298	A359KFA	Iveco 35.8	PMT	B14F	1984	
299	A360KFA	Iveco 35.8	PMT	B14F	1984	

300-327   Ford Transit 190   Robin Hood   B16F   1985

300	C862DYD	306	C868DYD	313	C875DYD	318	C880DYD	323	C885DYD
301	C863DYD	307	C869DYD	314	C876DYD	319	C881DYD	324	C886DYD
302	C864DYD	308	C870DYD	315	C877DYD	320	C882DYD	325	C887DYD
303	C865DYD	309	C871DYD	316	C878DYD	321	C883DYD	326	C888DYD
304	C866DYD	311	C873DYD	317	C879DYD	322	C884DYD	327	C889DYD
305	C867DYD	312	C874DYD						

328-374 — Ford Transit 190 — Robin Hood — B16F — 1986

328	C890GYD	338	C900GYD	348	C910GYD	357	C919GYD	366	C928GYD
329	C891GYD	339	C901GYD	349	C911GYD	358	C920GYD	367	C929GYD
330	C892GYD	340	C902GYD	350	C912GYD	359	C921GYD	368	C930GYD
331	C893GYD	341	C903GYD	351	C913GYD	360	C922GYD	369	C931GYD
332	C894GYD	342	C904GYD	352	C914GYD	361	C923GYD	370	C932GYD
333	C895GYD	343	C905GYD	353	C915GYD	362	C924GYD	371	C933GYD
334	C896GYD	344	C906GYD	354	C916GYD	363	C925GYD	372	C934GYD
335	C897GYD	345	C907GYD	355	C917GYD	364	C926GYD	373	C935GYD
336	C898GYD	346	C908GYD	356	C918GYD	365	C927GYD	374	C936GYD
337	C899GYD	347	C909GYD						

376-393 — Ford Transit 190 — Dormobile — B16F* — 1986 — *389-91 are B8FL

376	C938GYD	380	C942GYD	383	C945GYD	388	C950GYD	391	C953GYD
377	C939GYD	381	C943GYD	384	C946GYD	389	C951GYD	392	C954GYD
378	C940GYD	382	C944GYD	385	C947GYD	390	C952GYD	393	C955GYD
379	C941GYD								

394	C368GFJ	Ford Transit 190	Dormobile	B16F	1986	
396	A358KFA	Iveco 35.8	PMT	B14F	1984	
397	D112DRV	Iveco Daily 49.10	Robin Hood	B21F	1986	Ex People's Provincial

401-437 — Ford Transit 190 — Robin Hood — B16F — 1986

401	C54FDV	409	C330GFJ	416	C337GFJ	422	C343GFJ	432	C353GFJ
402	C55FDV	410	C331GFJ	417	C338GFJ	425	C346GFJ	434	C355GFJ
403	C56FDV	412	C333GFJ	418	C339GFJ	427	C348GFJ	435	C356GFJ
404	C325GFJ	413	C334GFJ	420	C341GFJ	428	C349GFJ	436	C357GFJ
405	C326GFJ	414	C335GFJ	421	C342GFJ	429	C350GFJ	437	C358GFJ
406	C327GFJ	415	C336GFJ						

438-446 — Ford Transit 190 — Dormobile — B16F — 1986 — 389-91 are B8FL

438	C359GFJ	440	C361GFJ	442	C363GFJ	444	C365GFJ	446	C367GFJ

447	C459BHY	Ford Transit 190	Dormobile	B16F	1986	Ex Bristol, 1989
448	C460BHY	Ford Transit 190	Dormobile	B16F	1986	Ex Bristol, 1989
449	C461BHY	Ford Transit 190	Dormobile	B16F	1986	Ex Bristol, 1989
451	B106XJO	Ford Transit 190	Carlyle	B16F	1985	Ex Devon General, 1992
452	B107XJO	Ford Transit 190	Carlyle	B16F	1985	Ex Devon General, 1992
453	B108XJO	Ford Transit 190	Carlyle	B16F	1985	Ex Devon General, 1992
454	B110XJO	Ford Transit 190	Carlyle	B16F	1985	Ex Devon General, 1992
506	D114DRV	Iveco Daily 49.10	Robin Hood	B21F	1986	Ex People's Provincial, 1989
507	D229VCD	Iveco Daily 49.10	Robin Hood	B21F	1987	Ex Brighton & Hove, 1989
508	D508OTA	Iveco Daily 49.10	Robin Hood	DP21F	1986	
509	D509OTA	Iveco Daily 49.10	Robin Hood	DP21F	1986	
510	D510OTA	Iveco Daily 49.10	Robin Hood	DP21F	1986	
511	D228VCD	Iveco Daily 49.10	Robin Hood	B21F	1987	Ex Brighton & Hove, 1989
512	D233VCD	Iveco Daily 49.10	Robin Hood	B21F	1987	Ex Brighton & Hove, 1989
513	D225VCD	Iveco Daily 49.10	Robin Hood	B21F	1987	Ex Brighton & Hove, 1989
514	D224VCD	Iveco Daily 49.10	Robin Hood	B21F	1987	Ex Brighton & Hove, 1989
520	D116DRV	Iveco Daily 49.10	Robin Hood	B21F	1986	Ex People's Provincial, 1989
522	E963HTP	Iveco Daily 49.10	Robin Hood	B25F	1987	Ex W & H, Horley, 1990
523	E640MBK	Iveco Daily 49.10	Robin Hood	B25F	1988	Ex W & H, Horley, 1990

524-528 — Iveco Daily 40.08 — Carlyle Dailybus 2 — B19F — 1989 — Ex East Midland, 1990

524	F908FHE	525	F905FHE	526	F906FHE	527	F907FHE	528	F909FHE

548	D548MJA	Iveco Daily 49.10	Robin Hood	B21F	1987	Ex GM Buses, 1990
549	D510MJA	Iveco Daily 49.10	Robin Hood	B21F	1987	Ex GM Buses, 1990
550	D550MJA	Iveco Daily 49.10	Robin Hood	B21F	1987	Ex GM Buses, 1990
555	ATA555L	Bristol VRT/SL2/6LX	Eastern Coach Works	O43/32F	1973	Ex Western National, 1983
559	ATA559L	Bristol VRT/SL2/6LX	Eastern Coach Works	O43/32F	1973	Ex Western National, 1983
574	VOD594S	Bristol VRT/SL3/6LXB	Eastern Coach Works	H43/31F	1978	Ex Western National, 1983

601-609	Bristol VRT/SL3/501	Eastern Coach Works	H43/31F*	1976	Ex Western National, 1983 *604-9 now Gardner engined

601	LWG844P	**604**	LWG847P	**606**	OWE849R	**608**	OWE851R	**609**	OWE852R
603	LWG846P	**605**	OWE848R	**607**	OWE850R				

701-710	Mercedes-Benz 709D	Carlyle	B29F	1991

701	H906WYB	**703**	H908WYB	**705**	H910WYB	**707**	H913WYB	**709**	H915WYB
702	H907WYB	**704**	H909WYB	**706**	H912WYB	**708**	H914WYB	**710**	H916WYB

711-718	Mercedes-Benz 709D	Wright	B29F	1992

711	J140SJT	**713**	J142SJT	**715**	J144SJT	**717**	J146SJT	**718**	J148SJT
712	J141SJT	**714**	J143SJT	**716**	J145SJT				

719	J969EYD	Mercedes-Benz 709D	Marshall	B29F	1992	
720	J241FYA	Mercedes-Benz 709D	Marshall	B29F	1992	
721	J580FYA	Mercedes-Benz 709D	Marshall	B29F	1992	
722	J601FYA	Mercedes-Benz 709D	Marshall	B29F	1992	
750	J610PTA	Mercedes-Benz 811D	Marshall	B33F	1992	
751	K751VFJ	Mercedes-Benz 811D	Wright Handybus	B33F	1992	
801	H801GDV	Dennis Dart 9.8SDL3012	Carlyle Dartline	B40F	1991	
802	H802GDV	Dennis Dart 9.8SDL3012	Carlyle Dartline	B40F	1991	
803	J803PFJ	Dennis Dart 9.8SDL3012	Wright Handybus	B39F	1992	
934	VDV134S	Bristol VRT/SL3/6LXB	Eastern Coach Works	CO43/31F	1977	Ex Devon General, 1983
942	VDV142S	Bristol VRT/SL3/6LXB	Eastern Coach Works	CO43/31F	1977	Ex Devon General, 1983
1056	OCK997K	Bristol VRT/SL6G	Eastern Coach Works	H39/31F	1972	Ex Crosville, 1987
1074	BFJ174L	Bristol VRT/SL2/6LX	Eastern Coach Works	H43/32F	1973	Ex Western National, 1983
1075	BFJ175L	Bristol VRT/SL2/6LX	Eastern Coach Works	H43/32F	1973	Ex Western National, 1983
1083	LOD723P	Bristol VRT/SL3/501	Eastern Coach Works	CH39/23F	1975	Ex Western National, 1983
1084	LOD724P	Bristol VRT/SL3/501	Eastern Coach Works	CH39/23F	1975	Ex Western National, 1983
1085	LOD725P	Bristol VRT/SL3/501	Eastern Coach Works	CH39/23F	1975	Ex Western National, 1983
1087	LOD727P	Bristol VRT/SL3/501	Eastern Coach Works	H43/32F	1975	Ex Western National, 1983

1093-1111	Bristol VRT/SL3/6LXB	Eastern Coach Works	H43/31F	1976-78	Ex Western National, 1983

1093	PTT93R	**1097**	PTT97R	**1102**	SFJ102R	**1110**	VDV110S	**1111**	VDV111S
1094	PTT94R	**1099**	PTT99R	**1109**	VDV109S				

1119	RTH926S	Bristol VRT/SL3/501	Eastern Coach Works	H43/31F	1977	Ex South Wales, 1988
1120	TWN939S	Bristol VRT/SL3/501	Eastern Coach Works	H43/31F	1977	Ex South Wales, 1988
1122	VDV122S	Bristol VRT/SL3/6LXB	Eastern Coach Works	H43/31F	1978	Ex Western National, 1983
1125	XDV605S	Bristol VRT/SL3/6LXB	Eastern Coach Works	H43/31F	1978	Ex Western National, 1983

1157-1193	Bristol VRT/SL3/6LXB	Eastern Coach Works	H43/31F	1979-80	Ex Western National, 1983

1157	AFJ764T	**1161**	AFJ768T	**1166**	AFJ773T	**1169**	FDV781V	**1173**	FDV785V
1158	AFJ765T	**1162**	AFJ769T	**1167**	FDV779V	**1170**	FDV782V	**1192**	FDV836V
1159	AFJ766T	**1165**	AFJ772T	**1168**	FDV780V	**1171**	FDV783V	**1193**	FDV837V
1160	AFJ767T								

1211	JFV311S	Leyland Atlantean AN68A/2R	East Lancashire	H50/36F	1978	Ex Blackpool, 1991
1212	JFV312S	Leyland Atlantean AN68A/2R	East Lancashire	H50/36F	1978	Ex Blackpool, 1991
1213	LFJ860W	Bristol VRT/SL3/6LXB	Eastern Coach Works	H43/31F	1981	Ex Devon General, 1990
1468	RDV419H	Bristol RELH6G	Eastern Coach Works	DP45F	1970	Ex Western National, 1983
1610	GDV459N	Bristol LH6L	Eastern Coach Works	B43F	1974	Ex Western National, 1983
1612	GPD317N	Bristol LHS6L	Eastern Coach Works	B35F	1974	Ex Busways, 1990
1613	AHT206J	Bristol RELL6L	Eastern Coach Works	B50F	1971	Ex Western National, 1990
1614	YHY596J	Bristol RELL6L	Eastern Coach Works	B50F	1971	Ex Western National, 1990
1615	YHY586J	Bristol RELL6L	Eastern Coach Works	B50F	1971	Ex Western National, 1990
1616	LHT173L	Bristol RELL6L	Eastern Coach Works	B50F	1973	Ex Western National, 1990
1634	REU326S	Bristol LH6L	Eastern Coach Works	B43F	1978	Ex Western National, 1983
1804	A680KDV	Leyland Olympian ONLXB/1R	Eastern Coach Works	H45/30F	1983	Ex Devon General, 1990
1805	A681KDV	Leyland Olympian ONLXB/1R	Eastern Coach Works	H45/30F	1983	Ex Devon General, 1990
1806	A682KDV	Leyland Olympian ONLXB/1R	Eastern Coach Works	H45/30F	1983	Ex Devon General, 1990
1809	UWW9X	Leyland Olympian ONLXB/1R	Roe	H47/29F	1982	Ex West Yorkshire PTE, 1987
1810	UWW10X	Leyland Olympian ONLXB/1R	Roe	H47/29F	1982	Ex West Yorkshire PTE, 1987
1811	A683KDV	Leyland Olympian ONLXB/1R	Eastern Coach Works	H45/30F	1983	Ex Devon General, 1990
1812	A684KDV	Leyland Olympian ONLXB/1R	Eastern Coach Works	H45/30F	1983	Ex Devon General, 1990
1813	A685KDV	Leyland Olympian ONLXB/1R	Eastern Coach Works	H45/30F	1983	Ex Devon General, 1990
1814	A686KDV	Leyland Olympian ONLXB/1R	Eastern Coach Works	H45/30F	1983	Ex Devon General, 1990
SN11	A580KVU	Leyland Tiger TRCTL11/3R	Plaxton Paramount 3200	C49F	1983	Ex Yelloway, Rochdale, 1985

SN12	620HOD	Leyland Tiger TRCTL11/3R	Plaxton Paramount 3500	C49F	1983	Ex Ambassador Travel, 1985
2221	FWH41Y	Leyland Tiger TRCTL11/3R	Plaxton Paramount 3200	C49F	1983	Ex Yelloway, Rochdale, 1985
2222	A68GBN	Leyland Tiger TRCTL11/3R	Plaxton Paramount 3200	C49F	1984	Ex Yelloway, Rochdale, 1985
2223	920GTA	Leyland Tiger TRCTL11/3RH	Plaxton Paramount 3200	C47FT	1985	
SN5	B895YYD	Leyland Tiger TRCTL11/3RH	Plaxton Paramount 3200	C48FT	1985	
2225	C923HYA	Leyland Tiger TRCTL11/3RZ	Plaxton Paramount 3500 II	C51F	1986	
2226	H226CFJ	Volvo B10M-60	Plaxton Expressliner	C46FT	1991	
2227	H227CFJ	Volvo B10M-60	Plaxton Expressliner	C46FT	1991	
2228	H228CFJ	Volvo B10M-60	Plaxton Expressliner	C46FT	1991	
2229	H229CFJ	Volvo B10M-60	Plaxton Expressliner	C46FT	1991	
2400	BDV400L	Bristol RELH6G	Plaxton Elite III	C51F	1973	Ex Western National, 1989
2402	BDV402L	Bristol RELH6G	Plaxton Elite III	C51F	1973	Ex Western National, 1989
2421	USV823	Bristol RELH6L	Plaxton Elite III	C51F	1974	Ex Western National, 1983
2429	GTA810N	Leyland Leopard PSU3B/4RT	Plaxton Elite III	C47F	1975	Ex Brutonian, 1991
2439	LOD720P	Leyland Leopard PSU3C/4RT	Plaxton Supreme III	C47F	1976	Ex Brutonian, 1991
2455	SFJ155R	Leyland Leopard PSU3E/4RT	Plaxton Supreme III	C47F	1977	Ex Western National, 1983
2810	THX187S	Leyland National 10351A/2R		B40F	1978	Ex Thames Transit, 1991
2811	THX220S	Leyland National 10351A/2R		B40F	1978	Ex Thames Transit, 1991
2812	WDR665M	Leyland National 1151/2R/0302		DP41F	1974	Ex Plymouth, 1989
2813	HTA844N	Leyland National 11351/1R		B49F	1975	Ex Western National, 1983
2814	MOD814P	Leyland National 11351/1R		B50F	1976	Ex Western National, 1983
2820	MOD820P	Leyland National 11351/1R		B50F	1976	Ex Western National, 1983
2821	MOD821P	Leyland National 11351/1R		B50F	1976	Ex Western National, 1983

2823-2882

Leyland National 11351A/1R — B50F — 1976-79 Ex Western National, 1983-91

2823	MOD823P	2850	PTT90R	2869	AFJ708T	2876	AFJ751T	2880	FDV776V
2828	MOD828P	2852	PTT75R	2871	AFJ710T	2878	FDV774V	2881	FDV777V
2829	MOD829P	2855	SFJ135R	2872	AFJ711T	2879	FDV775V	2882	FDV778V
2830	MOD852P	2868	AFJ707T						

2919	OJF419P	Leyland National 10351/1R		B41F	1976	Ex Country Bus, Atherington, 1990
3106	SFJ126R	Bristol LH6L	Plaxton Supreme III Exp	C41F	1977	Ex Country Bus, Atherington, 1990
3109	SFJ129R	Bristol LH6L	Plaxton Supreme III Exp	C41F	1977	Ex Country Bus, Atherington, 1990
3130	AFJ691T	Bristol LH6L	Plaxton Supreme III Exp	C41F	1977	Ex Western National, 1983
3133	AFJ694T	Bristol LH6L	Plaxton Supreme III Exp	C41F	1977	Ex Country Bus, Atherington, 1990

3303-3312

Bristol LH6L — Plaxton Supreme III Exp — C41F — 1979 — Ex Western National, 1983

3303	AFJ723T	3307	AFJ727T	3309	AFJ729T	3310	AFJ730T	3312	AFJ732T
3306	AFJ726T	3308	AFJ728T						

3313	RHE987R	Bristol LHS6L	Plaxton Supreme III Exp	C33F	1977	Ex Country Bus, Atherington, 1990
3314	AFJ734T	Bristol LH6L	Plaxton Supreme III Exp	C41F	1979	Ex Western National, 1983
3315	AFJ735T	Bristol LH6L	Plaxton Supreme III Exp	C41F	1979	Ex Western National, 1983
3400	PTT100R	Bristol LH6L	Plaxton Supreme III Exp	C43F	1976	Ex Western National, 1983
3410	SFJ110R	Bristol LH6L	Plaxton Supreme III Exp	C43F	1977	Ex Western National, 1983
3501	LTA731P	Leyland Leopard PSU3C/4RT	Plaxton Supreme III Exp	C49F	1976	Ex Western National, 1983
3506	SFJ134R	Leyland Leopard PSU3C/4RT	Plaxton Supreme III Exp	C49F	1977	Ex Western National, 1983
3507	SFJ157R	Leyland Leopard PSU3C/4RT	Plaxton Supreme III Exp	C49F	1977	Ex Western National, 1983

3512-3547

Leyland Leopard PSU3E/4R — Plaxton Supreme III Exp — C49F — 1978-80 Ex Western National, 1983
except 3540 ex Devon General, 1990 and 3547 ex Thames Transit, 1991

3512	VOD612S	3515	VOD615S	3521	AFJ713T	3526	AFJ718T	3541	KFX532V
3513	YTA792S	3520	AFJ712T	3525	AFJ717T	3540	FDV796V	3547	FDV803V

8001	EYP29V	Bedford YMT	Plaxton Supreme IV	C53F	1980	Ex Wahl, London SE5, 1984
8002	YNF348T	Bedford YMT	Plaxton Supreme IV	C53F	1978	Ex Richardson, Sheffield, 1987
8003	CMJ2T	Bedford YMT	Plaxton Supreme IV	C53F	1978	Ex Premier, Watford, 1986
8004	595JPU	Bedford YRT	Duple Dominant	C53F	1976	Ex Osmond, Curry Rivel, 1981
8005	NFH389P	Bedford YRT	Duple Dominant	C53F	1976	Ex Perrett, Shipton Oliffe, 1982
8006	865GAT	Bedford YRQ	Plaxton Elite III	C49F	1975	Ex Bicknell, Godalming, 1979
8007	KYC604N	Bedford YRQ	Plaxton Elite III	C49F	1975	Ex TRS, Leicester, 1987
8008	GJT951N	Bedford YRT	Plaxton Elite III	C53F	1975	Ex Pearce, Cattistock, 1978
8009	XJT205M	Bedford YRT	Plaxton Elite III	C53F	1973	Ex Browning, Box, 1987
8011	OFX110P	Bedford YRT	Plaxton Elite III	C53F	1973	Ex Allan, Foulden, 1982
8012	CAV624V	Volvo B58-56	Duple Dominant II	C53F	1979	Ex Smith, Portland, 1991
8013	KFX791	Leyland Tiger TRCTL11/3R	Plaxton Paramount 3200	C50F	1983	Ex Arlington demonstrator
8014	PUS157W	Leyland Leopard PSU3F/4R	Alexander AY	B53F	1981	Ex Smith, Portland, 1990
8015	G115JBO	Leyland Tiger TRCL10/3ARZH	Plaxton Paramount 3500 III	C45FT	1990	Ex Hills, Tredegar, 1991
8016	USV821	Leyland Tiger TRCTL11/3RH	Plaxton Paramount 3200	C46FT	1984	
8017	XOJ431T	Bedford YMT	Plaxton Supreme IV Exp	C53F	1978	Ex Bowen, Birmingham, 1991

8018	EUK547V	Bedford YMT	Plaxton Supreme IV Exp	C53F	1978	Ex Bowen, Birmingham, 1991
8019	XOJ432T	Bedford YMT	Plaxton Supreme IV Exp	C53F	1978	Ex Bowen, Birmingham, 1991
8020	EUK546V	Bedford YMT	Plaxton Supreme IV Exp	C53F	1978	Ex Bowen, Birmingham, 1991

Operating companies:

Comfylux:	281/98, 8001-18, SN12
Red Bus:	280, 401-10/2-40, 506-14, 712/7/8/50/1, 801-3, 1056/87/94/9, 1119/20/62/73, 1211-3, 1612, 1805/11/3, 2221-9, 2455, 2810-4/50/2/5/68/9/71/2/6/8/81/2, 2919, 3303/12-5, 3512/25, 3546.
Smith of Portland:	9, 412, 1613-6, 2402.
Southern National:	Remainder.

Previous Registrations:

595JPU	RBW176P	920GTA	B335WFJ	OFX110P	LGB750P, KFX791
620HOD	A897KCL	KFX532V	FDV797V, USV821	OJF419P	KBU893P, 5946PP
865GAT	LPA76P	KFX791	FNM854Y	USV821	A679KDV
YTA792S	VOD613S, 925GTA	KYC604N	JNR885N, 620HOD	USV823	RTT421N

Special Liveries:

Atlantic Blue:	2814/71/8/81/2.
Southern National:	750, 1094/9, 1119/62. 1211-3, 3312, 3512
Superbus:	1109, 3540
Tiverton & District:	512, 1120/73, 1805/11/3, 2810/1, 2919.
Western National Blue:	1613-6.
Overall Advertisements:	300, 401/8/18/28, 704, 1170, 2879

PLYMOUTH CITYBUS

1-85   Renault-Dodge S56   Reeve Burgess   B23F*   1986   *49-52 are DP23F

1	D101LTA	10	D110LTA	19	D119LTA	40	D140LTA	70	D170LTA
2	D102LTA	11	D111LTA	20	D120LTA	49	D149LTA	71w	D171LTA
3	D103LTA	12	D112LTA	22	D122LTA	51	D151LTA	72	D172LTA
4	D104LTA	13	D113LTA	24	D124LTA	52	D152LTA	75	D175LTA
5	D105LTA	14	D114LTA	25w	D125LTA	59	D159LTA	76	D176LTA
6	D106LTA	15	D115LTA	33	D133LTA	66w	D166LTA	80	D180LTA
7	D107LTA	16	D116LTA	36	D136LTA	68	D168LTA	82	D182LTA
8	D108LTA	17	D117LTA	37	D137LTA	69	D169LTA	85w	D185LTA
9	D109LTA	18	D118LTA						

101-110   Dennis Dart 9.8SDL3017   Plaxton Pointer   B40F   1992

101	K101SFJ	103	K103SFJ	105	K105SFJ	108	K108SFJ	110	K110SFJ
102	K102SFJ	104	K104SFJ	107	K107SFJ	109	K109SFJ		

115-135   Leyland Atlantean AN68A/1R   Roe   H43/28D*   1978-79   *131-5 are H43/31F

115	OCO115S	128	STK128T	130	STK130T	132	STK132T	134	STK134T
127	STK127T	129	STK129T	131	STK131T	133	STK133T	135	STK135T

136-161   Leyland Atlantean AN68B/1R   East Lancashire   H43/28D*   1979-80   *138/43 are H43/31F

136	VJY136T	142	VJY142V	147	VJY147V	152	ATK152W	157	ATK157W
137	VJY137V	143	VJY143V	148	ATK148W	153	ATK153W	158	ODV202W
138	VJY138V	144	VJY144V	149	ATK149W	154	ATK154W	159	ODV203W
139	VJY139V	145	VJY145V	150	ATK150W	155	ATK155W	160	ATK160W
140	VJY140V	146	VJY146V	151	ATK151W	156	ATK156W	161	ATK161W
141	VJY141V								

162-171   Leyland Atlantean AN68C/1R   East Lancashire   H43/31F   1981

162	TTT162X	164	TTT164X	166	TTT166X	168	TTT168X	170	TTT170X
163	TTT163X	165	TTT165X	167	TTT167X	169	TTT169X	171	TTT171X

175	B175VDV	Volvo Citybus B10M-56	East Lancashire	H43/35F	1984
176	B176VDV	Volvo Citybus B10M-56	East Lancashire	H43/35F	1984
177	H177GTT	Volvo Citybus B10M-60	East Lancashire	DPH48/30F	1991
178	H178GTT	Volvo Citybus B10M-60	East Lancashire	DPH48/30F	1991
201	H361BDV	Mercedes-Benz 709D	Wadham Stringer	B24F	1990
202	H362BDV	Mercedes-Benz 709D	Wadham Stringer	B24F	1990

203-225				Mercedes-Benz 709D		Reeve Burgess Beaver		B24F		1990-91	
203	H683BTA	208	J208KTT	213	J213KTT	217	J217KTT	221	J221KTT
204	H684BTA	209	J209KTT	214	J214KTT	218	J218KTT	223	J223KTT
205	J205KTT	210	J210KTT	215	J215KTT	219	J219KTT	224	J224KTT
206	J206KTT	211	J211KTT	216	J216KTT	220	J220KTT	225	J225KTT
207	J207KTT	212	J212KTT						

226-247				Mercedes-Benz 709D		Plaxton Beaver		B24F		1992	
226	K226SFJ	231	K231SFJ	235	K235SFJ	239	K239SFJ	244	K244SFJ
227	K227SFJ	232	K232SFJ	236	K236SFJ	241	K241SFJ	245	K245SFJ
228	K228SFJ	233	K233SFJ	237	K237SFJ	242	K242SFJ	246	K246SFJ
229	K229SFJ	234	K234SFJ	238	K238SFJ	243	K243SFJ	247	K247SFJ

340	F973HGE	Volvo B10M-60	Plaxton Paramount 3500 III	C49FT	1989	Ex Park, Hamilton, 1992
341	F968HGE	Volvo B10M-60	Plaxton Paramount 3500 III	C53F	1989	Ex Park, Hamilton, 1992
342	H828AHS	Volvo B10M-60	Plaxton Paramount 3500 III	C49FT	1990	Ex Park, Hamilton, 1992
343	J343KTT	Volvo B10M-60	Plaxton Paramount 3500 III	C49FT	1991	
344	H344EOD	Volvo B10M-60	Plaxton Paramount 3500 III	C53F	1991	
345	E567UHS	Volvo B10M-61	Plaxton Paramount 3500 III	C49FT	1987	Ex Park, Hamilton, 1992
346	F988HGE	Volvo B10M-60	Plaxton Paramount 3500 III	C49FT	1989	Ex Park, Hamilton, 1992
347	G347VTA	Volvo B10M-60	Plaxton Paramount 3500 III	C53F	1990	
348	G348VTA	Volvo B10M-60	Plaxton Paramount 3500 III	C53F	1990	
350	UJY932	Volvo B10M-61	Van Hool Alizée	C49FT	1984	Ex Park, Hamilton, 1988
352	KAD352V	Leyland Leopard PSU5C/4R	Plaxton Supreme IV	C57F	1980	Ex Western National, 1985
355	KAD355V	Leyland Leopard PSU5C/4R	Plaxton Supreme IV	C57F	1980	Ex Western National, 1985
358	MCO658	Leyland Titan PD2/12	MCW Orion	O30/26R	1956	

Previous Registrations:

UJY932	A602UGD, MCO658	MCO658	MCO658, ADV935A

Special Liveries:
Centenary: 358
Overall Advertisements: 6, 17, 115/30/3/4/7/40/2-4/53/6/62/6
Park & Ride: 211/2/9.

THAMESDOWN

7	SDW237Y	Dennis Lancet SD512	Wadham Stringer Vanguard	DP33F	1983	Ex Wealden, Tunbridge Wells, 1992
9	UPD269X	Dennis Lancet SD503	Wadham Stringer Vanguard	B45F	1982	Ex Wealden, Tunbridge Wells, 1991
10	PJU90W	Dennis Falcon SDA401	Duple Dominant	B51F	1981	Ex Leicester, 1987
11	XJF91Y	Dennis Falcon SDA406	Duple Dominant	B52F	1983	Ex Leicester, 1987
12	XJF92Y	Dennis Falcon SDA406	Duple Dominant	B52F	1983	Ex Leicester, 1987
13	XJF93Y	Dennis Falcon SDA406	Duple Dominant	B52F	1983	Ex Leicester, 1987
14	A94FRY	Dennis Falcon SDA412	Duple Dominant	B52F	1984	Ex Leicester, 1987
15	A95FRY	Dennis Falcon SDA412	Duple Dominant	B52F	1984	Ex Leicester, 1987
16	A96FRY	Dennis Falcon SDA412	Duple Dominant	B52F	1984	Ex Leicester, 1987
31	GHR301W	Leyland Leopard PSU3F/4R	Duple Dominant II Exp	C53F	1981	
33	SWW131R	Leyland Leopard PSU3E/4R	Duple Dominant II	C53F	1977	Ex Wallace Arnold, 1983
34	XWX174S	Leyland Leopard PSU3E/4R	Duple Dominant II	C53F	1978	Ex Wallace Arnold, 1986
35	XWX165S	Leyland Leopard PSU3E/4R	Duple Dominant II	C53F	1978	Ex AH, Leeds, 1985
36	EWW220T	Leyland Leopard PSU3E/4R	Duple Dominant II	C53F	1979	Ex Wallace Arnold, 1985
37	EWW221T	Leyland Leopard PSU3E/4R	Duple Dominant II	C53F	1979	Ex Wallace Arnold, 1985

50-58				Dennis Dominator DD152B*		Northern Counties		H43/31F		1982-83	*55-8 are DDA164
50	MHR50X	52	MHR52X	54	MHR54X	56	SMW56Y	58	SMW58Y
51	MHR51X	53	MHR53X	55	SMW55Y	57	SMW57Y		

59-63				Dennis Dominator DDA174		Northern Counties		H43/31F		1984	
59	A59WMM	60	A60WMM	61	A61WMM	62	A62WMM	63	A63WMM

64-68				Dennis Dominator DDA909		Northern Counties		DPH43/31F		1985	
64	B64GHR	65	B65GHR	66	B66GHR	67	B67GHR	68	B68GHR

69-73
Dennis Dominator DDA1033 — East Lancashire — H45/31F — 1990

69	H969XHR	70	H970XHR	71	H971XHR	72	H972XHR	73	H973XHR

101-110
Dennis Dart SDL3003 — Plaxton Pointer — B33F — 1993

101	K101OMW	103	K103OMW	105	K105OMW	107	K107OMW	109	K109OMW
102	K102OMW	104	K104OMW	106	K106OMW	108	K108OMW	110	K110OMW

125-136
Leyland Fleetline FE30AGR — MCW — H45/32F* — 1977 — Ex London Transport, 1983-5

125	OJD213R	127	OJD220R	129	OJD236R	134	OJD202R	136	OJD239R
126	OJD215R	128	OJD210R	130	OJD196R	135	OJD234R		

145	JAM145E	Daimler CVG6-30	Northern Counties	H40/30F	1967
175	KMW175P	Daimler Fleetline CRG6LX	Eastern Coach Works	O43/31F	1976

187-205
Leyland Fleetline FE30AGR — Eastern Coach Works — H43/31F — 1977-80

187	OHR187R	191	UMR191T	195	UMR195T	199	UMR199T	203	BMR203V
188	OHR187R	192	UMR192T	196	UMR196T	200	UMR200T	204	BMR204V
189	OHR187R	193	UMR193T	197	UMR197T	201	BMR201V	205	BMR205V
190	OHR190R	194	UMR194T	198	UMR198T	202	BMR202V		

206-219
Leyland Fleetline FE30AGR — Northern Counties — H43/32F — 1977-79 Ex GM Buses, 1988-89

206	PTD644S	200	ANA30T	212	BVR66T	215	PTD655S	218	TWH698T
207	PTD645S	210	XBU6S	213	BVR83T	216	BVR59T	219	TWH699T
208	XBU14S	211	XBU19S	214	ANA32T	217	BVR89T		

230-234
Dennis Dominator DD120A — East Lancashire — H43/32F — 1980 — Ex East Staffordshire, 1985

230	LBF230V	231	LBF231V	232	LBF232V	233	LBF233V	234	LBF234V

235	PRE37W	Dennis Dominator DD120A	East Lancashire	H43/32F	1981	Ex East Staffordshire, 1986
236	NRR106W	Dennis Dominator DD120A	Northern Counties	H43/30F	1981	Ex Derby, 1986
237	NRR107W	Dennis Dominator DD120A	Northern Counties	H43/30F	1981	Ex Derby, 1986
238	NRR108W	Dennis Dominator DD120A	Northern Counties	H43/30F	1981	Ex Derby, 1986
305	A305AHR	Leyland Tiger TRCTL11/2R	Duple Laser	C53F	1984	
306	A306AHR	Leyland Tiger TRCTL11/2R	Duple Laser	C53F	1984	
311	MIW3681	Leyland Tiger TRCTL11/3R	Duple Caribbean 2	C51F	1986	
313	MIW3783	Leyland Tiger TRCTL11/3RH	Duple Caribbean 2	C49FT	1986	Ex British Airways, 1988
314	MIW5844	Leyland Tiger TRCTL11/3RH	Duple Caribbean 2	C51FT	1986	Ex British Airways, 1988
316	B416CMC	Leyland Tiger TRCTL11/3R	Plaxton Paramount 3200	C57F	1985	Ex British Airways, 1988
317	A127EPA	Leyland Tiger TRCTL11/2R	Plaxton Paramount 3200	C53F	1985	Ex London Country NE, 1989
321	F321HHR	Dennis Javelin 12SDA1910	Duple 320	C53F	1989	
331	MJI6251	Scania K112TRB	Plaxton Paramount 4000 II	CH55/20DT	1986	Ex Marshall, Leighton Buzzard, 1990
332	XMW120	Scania K112TRB	Plaxton Paramount 4000 II	CH55/16DT	1986	Ex McColl, Balloch, 1992
333	GIL8493	Scania K112TRS	Berkhof Eclipse	CH55/16DT	1985	Ex King's Ferry, Gillingham, 1992
334	709LAU	Scania K112TRS	Berkhof Eclipse	CH57/19DT	1985	Ex King's Ferry, Gillingham, 1992
341	GIL8497	Volvo B10M-61	Berkhof Esprite 350	C49FT	1987	Ex King's Ferry, Gillingham, 1992
342	GIL8498	Volvo B10M-61	Berkhof Esprite 350	C49FT	1987	Ex King's Ferry, Gillingham, 1992
401	D401TMW	Renault-Dodge S56	Reeve Burgess	DP25F	1987	
402	E402WAM	Renault-Dodge S56	Reeve Burgess	DP25F	1988	
403	E403WAM	Renault-Dodge S56	Reeve Burgess	DP25F	1988	

404-414
Renault-Dodge S56 — Northern Counties — B25F* — 1988-90 411 ex NCME demonstrator, 1989
*412-4 are DP25F

404	E404YMR	407	E407YMR	409	E409YMR	411	E576ANE	413	G413OAM
405	E405YMR	408	E408YMR	410	E410YMR	412	G412OAM	414	G414OAM
406	E406YMR								

475	F75AKB	Renault-Dodge S75	Northern Counties	B31F	1989	Ex NCME demonstrator, 1990
890	CNA265Y	Ford Transit 190	Made-to-Measure	C12F	1983	Ex Kingston, Salisbury, 1991
891	B472SCG	Ford Transit 190	Tedd	C12C	1978	Ex Kingston, Winterslow, 1985
896	UOR968T	Ford R1114	Duple Dominant II	C53F	1980	Ex Corp, Fairoak, 1983
897	FHO86W	Ford R1114	Plaxton Supreme IV	C53F	1980	Ex Kingston, Salisbury, 1991
898	FOR398	Ford R1114	Plaxton Supreme V	C53F	1982	Ex Kingston, Salisbury, 1991
899	447ECR	Leyland Tiger TRCTL11/2R	Plaxton Supreme V	C53F	1982	Ex Kingston, Salisbury, 1991
900	964FYM	Leyland Tiger TRCTL11/3R	Plaxton Supreme V	C57F	1982	Ex Kingston, Salisbury, 1991
901	416YKO	Leyland Tiger TRCTL11/3R	Plaxton Supreme V	C57F	1982	Ex Kingston, Salisbury, 1991
902	B126PEL	Leyland Tiger TRCTL11/3R	Plaxton Paramount 3200	C53F	1985	Ex Kingston, Salisbury, 1991
903	C194WJT	Leyland Tiger TRCTL11/3RZ	Plaxton Paramount 3200 II	C53F	1986	Ex Kingston, Salisbury, 1991

904	C97NNV	Leyland Tiger TRCTL11/3R	Caetano Algarve	C53F	1986	Ex Kingston, Salisbury, 1991
905	C413LRP	Volvo B10M-61	Jonckheere Jubilee P50	C51FT	1985	Ex Kingston, Salisbury, 1991
906	D104ERU	Leyland Tiger TRCTL11/3RZ	Plaxton Paramount 3500 III	C57F	1987	Ex Kingston, Salisbury, 1991
907	E640NEL	Volvo B10M-61	Plaxton Paramount 3500 III	C53F	1987	Ex Kingston, Salisbury, 1991
908	E136PLJ	Dennis Javelin 12SDA1907	Plaxton Paramount 3200 III	C57F	1987	Ex Kingston, Salisbury, 1991
909	F909UPR	Volvo B10M-61	Plaxton Paramount 3500 III	C51FT	1988	Ex Kingston, Salisbury, 1991
910	E910UPR	Dennis Javelin 8SDL1903	Plaxton Paramount 3200 III	C33F	1989	Ex Kingston, Salisbury, 1991
911	F911YNV	Volvo B10M-61	Jonckheere Jubilee P50	C51FT	1988	Ex Kingston, Salisbury, 1991
912	G501VRV	Leyland Tiger TRCTL11/3ARZM	Plaxton Paramount 3500 III	C53F	1990	Ex Southampton, 1992
913	G138MNA	Volvo B10M-61	Jonckheere Deauville	C51FT	1990	Ex Buddens, 1992
914	F951RNV	Volvo B10M-61	Jonckheere Jubilee P50	C51FT	1989	Ex Amport & District, 1992

Special Liveries:
Overall Advertisements: 51/7, 68

Operations:	Kingston Coaches:	501, 890/1/6-911

Previous Registrations:

416YKO	KAA247Y	GIL8493	C112FMJ	MIW3783	C753FMC, XMW120
447ECR	UJT988X	GIL8497	E234AVX	MIW5844	C754FMC
709LAU	C276GVX	GIL8498	E235AVX	MJI6251	C351DWR
964FYM	VPR861X	MIW3681	C351LMR	XMW120	C213BOS, 13CLT,
FOR398	UFX632X				C919MGB

Named Vehicles:
64 *North Star*, 65 *City of Truro*, 66 *King George V*, 67 *Evening Star*, 68 *Western Enterprise*, 69 *Western Pathfinder*, 70 *Western Explorer*, 71 *Western Pioneer*, 72 *Western Crusader*, 73 *Western Venturer*, 175 *Isambard Kingdom Brunel*, 305 *Charles Saunders*, 306 *William Dean*, 311 *Sir Felix Pole*, 313 *Sir Daniel Gooch*, 314 *Sir James Milne*, 316 *Armstrong*, 317 *G J Churchward*, 321 *Viscount Churchill*, 331 *Great Western*, 332 *Lord of the Isles*, 333 *Iron Duke*, 334 *Tornado*, 341 *Charles J Hambro*, 342 *Viscount Portal*.

WESTERN NATIONAL

40	C201PCD	Mercedes-Benz L608D	Alexander AM	B20F	1985	Ex Brighton & Hove, 1990
41	C202PCD	Mercedes-Benz L608D	Alexander AM	B20F	1985	Ex Brighton & Hove, 1990
42	C211PCD	Mercedes-Benz L608D	Alexander AM	B20F	1985	Ex Brighton & Hove, 1990
50	B37AAF	Mercedes-Benz L608D	PMT	DP18F	1984	

51-56

		Mercedes-Benz L608D		Reeve Burgess	B19F*	1984	*54 is B14FL	
51	B38AAF	53	B40AAF	54	B41AAF	55	B42AAF	56	B43AAF
52	B39AAF							

57-126

		Mercedes-Benz L608D		Reeve Burgess	B20F*	1985-86	*80-5/117-26 are DP19F	
57	C672ECV	71	C689ECV	85	C700ECV	101	C798FRL	114	C957GAF
58	C673ECV	72	C684ECV	86	C783FRL	102	C799FRL	115	C958GAF
59	C674ECV	73	C685ECV	87	C784FRL	103	C800FRL	116	C959GAF
60	C675ECV	74	C686ECV	88	C785FRL	104	C801FRL	117	C963GCV
61	C676ECV	75	C690ECV	89	C786FRL	105	C802FRL	118	C964GCV
62	C677ECV	76	C691ECV	90	C787FRL	106	C949GAF	119	C965GCV
63	C678ECV	77	C692ECV	92	C789FRL	107	C950GAF	120	C966GCV
64	C679ECV	78	C693ECV	94	C791FRL	108	C951GAF	121	C967GCV
65	C680ECV	79	C694ECV	95	C792FRL	109	C952GAF	122	C968GCV
66	C681ECV	80	C695ECV	96	C793FRL	110	C953GAF	123	C969GCV
67	C682ECV	81	C696ECV	97	C794FRL	111	C954GAF	124	C970GCV
68	C683ECV	82	C697ECV	98	C795FRL	112	C955GAF	125	C489HCV
69	C687ECV	83	C698ECV	99	C796FRL	113	C956GAF	126	C491HCV
70	C688ECV	84	C699ECV	100	C797FRL				

127-132

		Mercedes-Benz L608D		PMT	B20F	1986		
127	C978GCV	129	C980GCV	130	C981GCV	131	C982GCV	132	C983GCV
128	C979GCV							

133-139

		Mercedes-Benz L608D		Robin Hood	B20F	1986		
133	C984GCV	135	C986GCV	137	C988GCV	138	C989GCV	139	C990GCV
134	C985GCV	136	C987GCV					

140	C229HCV	Mercedes-Benz L608D	Reeve Burgess	B20F	1986			
141	C230HCV	Mercedes-Benz L608D	Robin Hood	B20F	1986			
142	C231HCV	Mercedes-Benz L608D	Robin Hood	B20F	1986			
143	C232HCV	Mercedes-Benz L608D	Robin Hood	B20F	1986			
144	D534KGL	Mercedes-Benz L608D	Robin Hood	B20F	1986			

145-156

Mercedes-Benz L608D — Reeve Burgess — B20F — 1986

145	C98HGL	148	C101HGL	151	C104HGL	153	C106HGL	155	C108HGL
146	C99HGL	149	C102HGL	152	C105HGL	154	C107HGL	156	C109HGL
147	C100HGL	150	C103HGL						

157	E208BOD	Iveco Daily 49.10	Reeve Burgess Beaver	B21F	1988

200-205

Leyland Lynx LX112TL11R1R — Leyland — B51F — 1988

200	E200BOD	202	E202BOD	203	E203BOD	204	E204BOD	205	E205BOD
201	E201BOD							

301-326

Mercedes-Benz 811D — Carlyle — B31F* — 1990-91   *301/5/11 are DP31F

301	G151GOL	307	H892LOX	312	H712HGL	317	H717HGL	322	H722HGL
302	G152GOL	308	H893LOX	313	H713HGL	318	H718HGL	323	H723HGL
303	G153GOL	309	H894LOX	314	H714HGL	319	H719HGL	324	H724HGL
304	G154GOL	310	H895LOX	315	H715HGL	320	H720HGL	325	H725HGL
305	G155GOL	311	H896LOX	316	H716HGL	321	H721HGL	326	H726HGL
306	H891LOX							

327	E807MOU	Mercedes-Benz 811D	Optare StarRider	B31F	1988	Ex Badgerline, 1991
328	E808MOU	Mercedes-Benz 811D	Optare StarRider	B31F	1988	Ex Badgerline, 1991
329	E812MOU	Mercedes-Benz 811D	Optare StarRider	B31F	1988	Ex Badgerline, 1991
330	E820MOU	Mercedes-Benz 811D	Optare StarRider	B31F	1988	Ex Badgerline, 1991

331-343

Mercedes-Benz 814D — Plaxton Beaver — B31F — 1992

331	K331NAF	334	K334NAF	337	K337NAF	340	K340NAF	342	K342NAF
332	K332NAF	335	K335NAF	338	K338NAF	341	K341NAF	343	K343NAF
333	K333NAF	336	K336NAF	339	K339NAF				

500	C488BFB	Ford Transit 190	Dormobile	B16F	1986	Ex Badgerline, 1991
501	C501BFB	Ford Transit 190	Dormobile	B16F	1986	Ex Badgerline, 1991
502	C524BFB	Ford Transit 190	Dormobile	B16F	1986	Ex Badgerline, 1991
503	B476YEU	Ford Transit 190	Dormobile	DP16F	1985	Ex Badgerline, 1991
518	D44OYA	Fiat 35.8	G&M	C14F	1987	Ex Robert's, Plympton, 1988
519	D45OYA	Fiat 35.8	G&M	C14F	1987	Ex Robert's, Plympton, 1988
524	E683XVU	Ford Transit 190	Deansgate	B12F	1988	
525	F999UGL	Ford Transit 190	Deansgate	B12F	1988	
526	F21URL	Ford Transit 190	Deansgate	B12F	1988	
550	F22URL	Ford Transit 190	Deansgate	B12F	1988	
552	A992SGK	Fiat 79F.10	Harwin	C22FT	1983	Ex Robert's, Plympton, 1988
553	LFR293X	Fiat 79F.10	Harwin	C29F	1982	Ex Robert's, Plympton, 1988
555	WDR274V	Fiat 55F.10	Harwin	C25F	1980	Ex Robert's, Plympton, 1988
557	C159DWT	Fiat 79.14	Caetano Viana	C19F	1986	Ex Robert's, Plympton, 1988
559	YFP429Y	Fiat 60F.10	Caetano Viana	C18F	1982	Ex Robert's, Plympton, 1988
565	PRF361W	Fiat 60F.10	Harwin	C25F	1981	Ex Robert's, Plympton, 1988
567	B674CBD	Fiat 60F.10	Caetano Viana	C18F	1984	Ex Robert's, Plympton, 1988
933	PPH463R	Bristol VRT/SL3/501 (Gardner)	Eastern Coach Works	H43/31F	1977	Ex Badgerline, 1989
934	PPH461R	Bristol VRT/SL3/501 (Gardner)	Eastern Coach Works	H43/31F	1977	Ex Badgerline, 1989
935	PPH466R	Bristol VRT/SL3/501	Eastern Coach Works	H43/31F	1977	Ex Badgerline, 1989
936	PPH467R	Bristol VRT/SL3/501 (Gardner)	Eastern Coach Works	H43/31F	1977	Ex Badgerline, 1989
941	VDV141S	Bristol VRT/SL3/6LXB	Eastern Coach Works	CO43/31F	1978	
943	VDV143S	Bristol VRT/SL3/6LXB	Eastern Coach Works	CO43/31F	1978	
944	VDV144S	Bristol VRT/SL3/6LXB	Eastern Coach Works	CO43/31F	1978	
1077	BFJ177L	Bristol VRT/SL2/6LX	Eastern Coach Works	H43/32F	1973	
1081	GTA51N	Bristol VRT/SL2/6LX	Eastern Coach Works	H43/32F	1975	
1083	JNU138N	Bristol VRT/SL2/6LX	Eastern Coach Works	H39/31F	1975	Ex Badgerline, 1988
1084	HTC728N	Bristol VRT/SL2/6LX	Eastern Coach Works	H39/31F	1975	Ex Badgerline, 1988
1085	KOU796P	Bristol VRT/SL3/6LXB	Eastern Coach Works	H39/31F	1976	Ex Badgerline, 1988
1086	MUA873P	Bristol VRT/SL3/6LX	Eastern Coach Works	H43/31F	1975	Ex Badgerline, 1989
1087	BEP968V	Bristol VRT/SL3/501 (Gardner)	Eastern Coach Works	H43/31F	1979	Ex South Wales, 1989
1095	PTT95R	Bristol VRT/SL3/6LXB	Eastern Coach Works	H43/31F	1976	

1100-1108

Bristol VRT/SL3/6LXB — Eastern Coach Works — H43/31F — 1977 — 1101/3/5 ex Devon General, 1987

1100 SFJ100R	1103 SFJ103R	1106 SFJ106R	1107 SFJ107R	1108 VDV108S
1101 SFJ101R	1105 SFJ105R			

1109	UTO832S	Bristol VRT/SL3/501(Gardner)	Eastern Coach Works	H43/31F	1977 Ex Devon General, 1987
1111	UTO836S	Bristol VRT/SL3/501(Gardner)	Eastern Coach Works	H43/31F	1977 Ex Devon General, 1987

1114-1131

Bristol VRT/SL3/6LXB — Eastern Coach Works — H43/31F — 1977-78

1114 VDV114S	1117 VDV117S	1120 VDV120S	1128 XDV608S	1130 XDV600S
1115 VDV115S	1118 VDV118S	1121 VDV121S	1129 XDV609S	1131 XDV601S
1116 VDV116S	1119 VDV119S	1123 XDV603S		

1132-1220

Bristol VRT/SL3/6LXB — Eastern Coach Works — H43/31F — 1978-81

1132 AFJ697T	1140 AFJ705T	1148 AFJ750T	1156 AFJ763T	1198 LFJ842W
1133 AFJ698T	1141 AFJ706T	1149 AFJ751T	1174 FDV806V	1199 LFJ843W
1134 AFJ699T	1142 AFJ744T	1150 AFJ752T	1175 FDV807V	1200 LFJ844W
1135 AFJ700T	1143 AFJ745T	1151 AFJ753T	1176 FDV808V	1201 LFJ845W
1136 AFJ701T	1144 AFJ746T	1152 AFJ759T	1182 FDV814V	1202 LFJ846W
1137 AFJ702T	1145 AFJ747T	1153 AFJ760T	1183 FDV815V	1203 LFJ847W
1138 AFJ703T	1146 AFJ748T	1154 AFJ761T	1197 LFJ841W	1220 LFJ867W
1139 AFJ704T	1147 AFJ749T	1155 AFJ762T		

1224	LFJ871W	Bristol VRT/SL3/6LXC	Eastern Coach Works	H43/31F	1981
1225	LFJ872W	Bristol VRT/SL3/6LXC	Eastern Coach Works	H43/31F	1981
1226	LFJ873W	Bristol VRT/SL3/6LXC	Eastern Coach Works	H43/31F	1981
1227	EWS747W	Bristol VRT/SL3/680(Gardner)	Eastern Coach Works	DPH43/31F	1981 Ex Badgerline, 1990

1228-1237

Bristol VRT/SL3/501* — Eastern Coach Works — H43/31F — 1977-79 Ex South Wales, 1990
*1228 now Gardner engine.

1228 RTH929S	1230 VTH942T	1232 WTH945T	1234 WTH950T	1236 WTH961T
1229 TWN936S	1231 WTH943T	1233 WTH946T	1235 WTH951T	1237 BEP966V

1238-1251

Bristol VRT/SL3/6LXB* — Eastern Coach Works — H43/31F — 1976-81 Ex Thamesway, 1991-92
1247 is VRT/SL3/501(Gardner); 1238 is H39/31F

1238 KOO785V	1241 XHK231X	1244 UAR589W	1247 OBD841P	1250 XHK220X
1239 UAR595W	1242 XHK228X	1245 UAR594W	1248 UAR590W	1251 XHK230X
1240 XHK225X	1243 UAR586W	1246 UAR597W	1249 XHK223X	

1400	E213BOD	Aüwaerter Neoplan N122/3	Aüwaerter Skyliner	CH57/20CT	1988	
1401	E214BOD	Aüwaerter Neoplan N122/3	Aüwaerter Skyliner	CH57/20CT	1988	
1421	C979HOX	MCW Metroliner DR131/31	MCW	CH55/17DT	1986	Ex Midland Red West, 1989
1558	FDV788V	Bristol LHS6L	Eastern Coach Works	B35F	1979	
1565	KRL444W	Bristol LHS6L	Wadham Stringer Vanguard	B35F	1981	Ex Grenville, Truro, 1988
1566	PCV178R	Bristol LHS6L	Marshall	B34F	1977	Ex Grenville, Truro, 1988
1568	HDL414N	Bristol LHS6L	Eastern Coach Works	B35F	1975	Ex United, 1988
1569	SNU389R	Bristol LHS6L	Eastern Coach Works	B35F	1976	Ex United, 1988
1617	PDD101M	Leyland Leopard PSU3B/4R	Duple Dominant	C47F	1974	Ex Midland Red West, 1988

1800-1810

Leyland Olympian ONLXB/1R — Eastern Coach Works — DPH44/32F — 1983

1800 A750VAF	1802 A752VAF	1807 A754VAF	1809 A756VAF	1810 A757VAF
1801 A751VAF	1803 A753VAF	1808 A755VAF		

2200	FDZ980	Leyland Tiger TRCTL11/3R	Duple Goldliner	C51F	1982	Ex United Welsh, 1991
2201	FDZ983	Leyland Tiger TRCTL11/3R	Duple Goldliner	C51F	1982	Ex United Welsh, 1991
2202	FDZ984	Leyland Tiger TRCTL11/3R	Duple Goldliner	C51F	1982	Ex Brewers, 1991
2203	A749VAF	Leyland Tiger TRCTL11/3R	Plaxton Paramount 3500	C46FT	1984	
2206	A530WRL	Leyland Tiger TRCTL11/3RH	Plaxton Paramount 3200	C46FT	1984	
2208	A532WRL	Leyland Tiger TRCTL11/3RH	Plaxton Paramount 3200	C46FT	1984	
2217	B194BAF	Leyland Tiger TRCTL11/3RH	Plaxton Paramount 3200 II	C48FT	1985	
2218	B195BAF	Leyland Tiger TRCTL11/3RH	Plaxton Paramount 3200 II	C48FT	1985	
2219	B196BAF	Leyland Tiger TRCTL11/3RH	Plaxton Paramount 3200 II	C48FT	1985	
2220	B197BAF	Leyland Tiger TRCTL11/3RH	Plaxton Paramount 3200 II	C48FT	1985	
2228	C974GCV	Leyland Tiger TRCTL11/3RZ	Duple 340	C46FT	1986	
2229	C975GCV	Leyland Tiger TRCTL11/3RZ	Duple 340	C46FT	1986	
2230	C976GCV	Leyland Tiger TRCTL11/3RZ	Duple 340	C46FT	1986	
2231	C977GCV	Leyland Tiger TRCTL11/3RZ	Duple 340	C46FT	1986	
2232	E978WTA	DAF MB230DKFL600	Duple 340	C53FT	1987	

2233	E339WTT	DAF MB230DKFL600	Duple 340	C53FT	1987	
2234	E340WTT	DAF MB230DKFL600	Duple 340	C53FT	1987	
2235	E341WTT	DAF MB230DKFL615	Duple 340	C53FT	1987	
2236	E342WTT	DAF MB230DKFL615	Duple 340	C53FT	1987	
2237	C792MVH	DAF MB200DKFL600	Plaxton Paramount 3500 II	C53F	1986	Ex Fishwick, Leyland, 1987
2239	A747JAY	Volvo B10M-61	Duple Caribbean	C49FT	1984	Ex Grenville, Truro, 1988
2240	E206BOD	Hestair Duple 425	Duple 425	C54FT	1988	
2241	E207BOD	Hestair Duple 425	Duple 425	C53FT	1988	
2242	E218CFJ	Hestair Duple 425	Duple 425	C53FT	1988	
2243	J243LGL	Volvo B10M-60	Plaxton Expressliner	C46FT	1992	
2244	J244LGL	Volvo B10M-60	Plaxton Expressliner	C46FT	1992	
2245	J245LGL	Volvo B10M-60	Plaxton Expressliner	C46FT	1992	
2246	J246LGL	Volvo B10M-60	Plaxton Expressliner	C46FT	1992	
2247	F444DUG	Volvo B10M-61	Plaxton Paramount 3500 III	C49FT	1989	Ex Wallace Arnold, 1992
2248	F446DUG	Volvo B10M-61	Plaxton Paramount 3500 III	C49FT	1989	Ex Wallace Arnold, 1992
2402	ETH68V	Leyland Leopard PSU3E/4R	Plaxton Supreme	C49F	1980	Ex South Wales, 1991
2425	GTA806N	Leyland Leopard PSU3B/4R	Plaxton Supreme (1977)	C51F	1975	Ex Devon General, 1988
2427	GTA808N	Leyland Leopard PSU3B/4R	Plaxton Elite III	C47F	1975	
2440	SFJ140R	Leyland Leopard PSU3E/4RT	Plaxton Supreme III	C47F	1976	
2444	SFJ144R	Leyland Leopard PSU3E/4RT	Plaxton Supreme III	C47F	1976	
2450	SFJ150R	Leyland Leopard PSU3E/4R	Plaxton Supreme III	C47F	1976	
2452	RRL375S	Leyland Leopard PSU3C/4R	Plaxton Supreme III	C47F	1977	Ex Grenville, Truro, 1987
2453	CPT823S	Leyland Leopard PSU3E/4R	Plaxton Supreme III	C47F	1978	Ex Grenville, Truro, 1987
2461	MPH5W	Ford R1114	Plaxton Supreme IV	C47F	1981	Ex Plympton Coachlines, 1987
2463	HFX424V	Ford R1114	Plaxton Supreme IV	C47F	1980	Ex Plympton Coachlines, 1987
2508	D508HHW	Volvo B10M-61	Van Hool Alizée	C48FT	1987	Ex Badgerline, 1992
2509	D509HHW	Volvo B10M-61	Van Hool Alizée	C48FT	1987	Ex Badgerline, 1992
2511	D511HHW	Volvo B10M-61	Van Hool Alizée	C48FT	1987	Ex Badgerline, 1992
3300	AFJ720T	Bristol LH6L	Plaxton Supreme III Exp	C41F	1979	
3301	AFJ721T	Bristol LH6L	Plaxton Supreme III Exp	C41F	1979	
3500	KTT808P	Leyland Leopard PSU3C/4RT	Plaxton Supreme III Exp	DP53F	1975	
3505	LTA735P	Leyland Leopard PSU3C/4RT	Plaxton Supreme III Exp	C49F	1975	
3508	SFJ158R	Leyland Leopard PSU3C/4R	Plaxton Supreme III Exp	C49F	1977	

3516-3524

				Leyland Leopard PSU3E/4RT	Plaxton Supreme III Exp	C49F	1978-79

3516	VOD616S	3518	VOD618S	3522	AFJ714T	3523	AFJ715T	3524	AFJ716T
3517	VOD617S	3519	YDV189S						

3530	FDV821V	Leyland Leopard PSU3E/4R	Willowbrook 003	C49F	1980
3535	FDV826V	Leyland Leopard PSU3E/4R	Willowbrook 003	C49F	1980
3537	FDV828V	Leyland Leopard PSU3E/4R	Willowbrook 003	C49F	1980

3538-3546

				Leyland Leopard PSU3E/4RT	Plaxton Supreme IV Exp	C46FT*	1978-79 3545/9 are C49F

3538	FDV794V	3542	FDV798V	3544	FDV800V	3545	FDV801V	3546	FDV802V

3549	FDV805V	Leyland Leopard PSU3F/4RT	Plaxton Supreme IV Exp	C49F	1980

Previous Registrations:

A992SGK	AEH632Y		FDZ980	OHM832Y		FDZ984	OHM831Y
ETH68V	KUB669V, 278TNY		FDZ983	LYW830X			

Special Liveries:

Blue Bus: 1565/6
Dartmouth Park & Ride: 157
Grenville: 2220, 2239, 2402/52/3, 3544
Plympton Coachlines: 2461/3
Overall Advertisements: 50/9, 81/9, 120/5/6, 1083/100/7/21/31/40/8, 1227.
Robert's Coaches: 54, 124, 500/3/18/9/24-6/50/2/3/5/7/9/65/7.

WILTS & DORSET

Note: vehicles commencing 4xxx are allocated to the low cost unit.

2301-2350   MCW MetroRider MF150   MCW   B23F   1987-88

2301	E452MEL	2311	E462MEL	2321	E472MEL	2331	E482MEL	2341	E492MEL
2302	E453MEL	2312	E463MEL	2322	E473MEL	2332	E483MEL	2342	E493MEL
2303	E454MEL	2313	E464MEL	2323	E474MEL	2333	E484MEL	2343	E494MEL
2304	E455MEL	2314	E465MEL	2324	E475MEL	2334	E485MEL	2344	E495MEL
2305	E456MEL	2315	E466MEL	2325	E476MEL	2335	E486MEL	2345	E496MEL
2306	E457MEL	2316	E467MEL	2326	E477MEL	2336	E487MEL	2346	E346REL
2307	E458MEL	2317	E468MEL	2327	E478MEL	2337	E488MEL	2347	E347REL
2308	E459MEL	2318	E469MEL	2328	E479MEL	2338	E489MEL	2348	E348REL
2309	E460MEL	2319	E470MEL	2329	E480MEL	2339	E490MEL	2349	E349REL
2310	E461MEL	2320	E471MEL	2330	E481MEL	2340	E491MEL	2350	E350REL

2351-2375   MCW MetroRider MF150   MCW   B23F   1989

2351	F351URU	2356	F356URU	2361	F361URU	2366	F366URU	2371	F371URU
2352	F352URU	2357	F357URU	2362	F362URU	2367	F367URU	2372	F372URU
2353	F353URU	2358	F358URU	2363	F363URU	2368	F368URU	2373	F373URU
2354	F354URU	2359	F359URU	2364	F364URU	2369	F369URU	2374	F374URU
2355	F355URU	2360	F360URU	2365	F365URU	2370	F370URU	2375	F375URU

2376	E613FRN	MCW MetroRider MF150/42	MCW	B23F	1987	Ex Blackburn, 1991

2377-2382   MCW MetroRider MF150   MCW   B23F   1987   Ex Grimsby-Cleethorpes, 1991

2377	E43HFE	2379	E52HFE	2380	E53HFE	2381	E54HFE	2382	E55HFE
2378	E44HFE							

2383-2388   MCW MetroRider MF150/34   MCW   B23F   1987   Ex Yorkshire Rider, 1991

2383	E227PWY	2385	E229PWY	2386	E230PWY	2387	E226PWY	2388	E233PWY
2384	E228PWY							

2501-2533   Optare MetroRider   Optare   B31F   1992

2501	J501RPR	2508	J508RPR	2515	J515RPR	2522	K522UJT	2528	K528UJT
2502	J502RPR	2509	J509RPR	2516	K516UJT	2523	K523UJT	2529	K529UJT
2503	J503RPR	2510	J510RPR	2517	K517UJT	2524	K524UJT	2530	K530UJT
2504	J504RPR	2511	J511RPR	2518	K518UJT	2525	K525UJT	2531	K531UJT
2505	J505RPR	2512	J512RPR	2519	K519UJT	2526	K526UJT	2532	K532UJT
2506	J506RPR	2513	J513RPR	2520	K520UJT	2527	K527UJT	2533	K533UJT
2507	J507RPR	2514	J514RPR	2521	K521UJT				

3059	NEL114P	Leyland Leopard PSU3C/4R	Plaxton Supreme III	C49F	1976	Ex Shamrock & Rambler, 1984
3069	BJT323T	Leyland Leopard PSU3E/4R	Plaxton Supreme III	C49F	1979	Ex Shamrock & Rambler, 1984

3201-3210   Leyland Tiger TRCTL11/3RH   Duple Laser 2   C53F   1984   3201-4 TRCTL11/3RZ, C51F

3201	B201REL	3203	B203REL	3205	B205REL	3207	B207REL	3209	B209REL
3202	B202REL	3204	B204REL	3206	B206REL	3208	B208REL	3210	B210REL

3307-3334   Bristol VRT/SL2/6LX   Eastern Coach Works   H43/31F   1974-75   Ex Hants & Dorset, 1983
*3308 ex Hampshire Bus, 1983

4308	NRU307M	4325	JJT437N	4327	JJT439N	4329	JJT441N	3334	JJT446N
4324	JJT436N	4326	JJT438N	4328	JJT440N	3332	JJT444N		

3335-3349   Bristol VRT/SL3/6LX   Eastern Coach Works   H43/31F   1976   Ex Hants & Dorset, 1983

4335	MEL556P	4337	MEL558P	4340	MEL561P	4348	NJT34PT	4349	NJT35P
4336	MEL557P	4339	MEL560P	4341	MEL562P				

3350-3356   Bristol VRT/SL3/501   Eastern Coach Works   H43/31F   1976   Ex Hants & Dorset, 1983
*3351 is O43/31F

3350	OEL231P	3352	OEL233P	3354	OEL235P	3355	OEL236P	3356	OEL237P
3351	OEL232P	3353	OEL234P						

3367-3456 Bristol VRT/SL3/6LXB Eastern Coach Works H43/31F 1977-80 Ex Hants & Dorset, 1983

3424 was rebodied 1980

3367	RJT158R	3399	YEL371T	3413	BFX666T	3425	ELJ217V	3436	GEL686V
4368	RJT159R	3400	BFX568T	3414	UDL671S	3426	ELJ218V	3437	GEL687V
3380	URU687S	3401	BFX569T	3415	UDL672S	3427	ELJ219V	3448	KRU848W
3381	URU688S	3403	BFX571T	3416	UDL673S	3428	ELJ220V	3449	KRU849W
3382	URU689S	3404	BFX572T	3417	UDL674S	3429	GEL679V	3450	KRU850W
3383	URU690S	3405	BFX573T	3418	UDL675S	3430	GEL680V	3451	KRU851W
4384	URU691S	3406	BFX574T	3419	UDL676S	3431	GEL681V	3453	KRU853W
4385	VPR484S	3407	BFX575T	3422	ELJ214V	3432	GEL682V	3454	KRU854W
4386	VPR485S	3411	BFX664T	3423	ELJ215V	3433	GEL683V	3455	KRU855W
4398	YEL5T	3412	BFX665T	3424	ELJ216V	3435	GEL685V	3456	KRU856W

3457	NUM340V	Bristol VRT/SL3/6LXB	Eastern Coach Works	H43/31F	1980	Ex Keighley & District, 1991
3458	JWT756V	Bristol VRT/SL3/6LXB	Eastern Coach Works	H43/31F	1979	Ex Keighley & District, 1991
3459	JWT759V	Bristol VRT/SL3/6LXB	Eastern Coach Works	H43/31F	1979	Ex Keighley & District, 1991
3645	GLJ681N	Leyland National 11351/1R		B49F	1975	Ex Hants & Dorset, 1983

3696-3751 Leyland National 11351A/1R B49F* 1977-79 Ex Hants & Dorset, 1983

*3726-30 are DP48F

3717	VFX983S	3727	TEL493R	3738	BEL730T	3740	BEL732T	3745	FPR61V
4722	VFX988S	3730	WFX255S	3739	BEL731T	3744	EEL894V	3751	FPR67V
3726	TEL492R	3736	XFX897S						

3763	VNO738S	Leyland National 11351A/1R	B49F	1977	Ex Eastern National 1986

3849-3858 Bristol LH6L Eastern Coach Works B43F 1980 Ex Hants & Dorset, 1983

3849	AFB585V	3852	AFB588V	3855	AFB591V	3856	AFB592V	3858	AFB595V
3851	AFB587V	3854	AFB590V						

3901-3905 Leyland Olympian ONLXB/1R Eastern Coach Works DPH42/28F 1984

3901	A901JPR	3902	A902JPR	3903	A903JPR	3904	A904JPR	3905	A905JPR

3906	A989XAF	Leyland Olympian ONLXB/1R	Eastern Coach Works	CO45/30F	1984	Ex Red Bus, 1986
3907	A990XAF	Leyland Olympian ONLXB/1R	Eastern Coach Works	CO45/30F	1984	Ex Red Bus, 1986

3908-3912 Leyland Olympian ONLXB/1R Roe CO47/29F 1982-84 Ex West Yorkshire PTE, 1987

3908	UWW12X	3909	UWW17X	3910	CUB67Y	3911	CUB70Y	3912	EWY80Y

3913	UWW16X	Leyland Olympian ONLXB/1R	Roe	H47/29F	1982	Ex Metrobus, Orpington, 1989

3914-3920 Leyland Olympian ONTL11/1R Roe H43/29F 1983-84 Ex County, Harlow, 1990

3914	A144DPE	3916	A156FPG	3918	A158FPG	3919	A159FPG	3920	A160FPG
3915	A145DPE								

3921	A173VFM	Leyland Olympian ONLXB/1R	Eastern Coach Works	H45/32F	1984	Ex Crosville Wales, 1990
3922	A174VFM	Leyland Olympian ONLXB/1R	Eastern Coach Works	H45/32F	1984	Ex Crosville Wales, 1990
3923	A175VFM	Leyland Olympian ONLXB/1R	Eastern Coach Works	H45/32F	1984	Ex Crosville Wales, 1990
3924	TTT172X	Leyland Olympian ONLXB/1R	East Lancashire	H43/31F	1982	Ex Stevensons, Uttoxeter, 1991
3925	TTT173X	Leyland Olympian ONLXB/1R	East Lancashire	H43/31F	1982	Ex Stevensons, Uttoxeter, 1991
3926	TTT174X	Leyland Olympian ONLXB/1R	East Lancashire	H43/31F	1982	Ex Stevensons, Uttoxeter, 1991
3927	UWW6X	Leyland Olympian ONLXB/1R	Roe	H47/29F	1982	Ex Stevensons, Uttoxeter, 1991
4001	XLS228A	Bristol Lodekka FS6G	Eastern Coach Works	CO33/27R	1961	Ex Hampshire Bus, 1992

Special Liveries:
Guide Friday: 3332/4
National Express: 3201-4/7/8.
Verwood Transport: 4384
Overall Advertisements: 2356/7, 3412/37

Previous Registrations:
XLS228A   866NHT

YELLOW BUSES

3	RIB8743	Leyland Tiger TRCTL11/3R	Plaxton Paramount 3500	C51F	1984	
4	RIB8744	Leyland Tiger TRCTL11/3R	Plaxton Paramount 3500	C50F	1984	Ex Travellers, Hounslow, 1984
5	RIB8745	Leyland Tiger TRCTL11/3RH	Plaxton Paramount 3500	C53F	1985	
6	RIB8746	Leyland Tiger TRCTL11/3RH	Plaxton Paramount 3500	C53F	1985	
7	RIB8747	DAF MB230LB615	Plaxton Paramount 3500	C51FT	1988	Ex Land Tourers, Farnham, 1991
8	RIB8748	DAF MB230LB615	Plaxton Paramount 3500 III	C51FT	1990	Ex Smith, Alcester, 1991
9	RIB8749	DAF MB230LB615	Plaxton Paramount 3500 III	C47FT	1991	
86	E786EGX	Peugeot-Talbot Express	Crystals	C14F	1988	Ex Raff, Gravesend, 1991
90	ERU390V	Leyland Leopard PSU3E/4R	Plaxton Supreme IV	DP51F	1979	
91	ERU391V	Leyland Leopard PSU3E/4R	Plaxton Supreme IV	DP51F	1979	
92	ERU392V	Leyland Leopard PSU3E/4R	Plaxton Supreme IV	DP51F	1979	
108	ERU108V	Leyland Leopard PSU3E/4R	Plaxton Supreme IV	C51F	1979	
109	JLJ109V	Leyland Leopard PSU3E/4R	Plaxton Supreme IV	C51F	1980	

121-129

Daimler Fleetline CRL6-30 — Alexander AL — H43/31F — 1974

121	OEL121M	123	OEL123M	125	OEL125M	127	OEL127M	129	OEL129M
122	OEL122M	124	OEL124M	126	OEL126M	128	OEL128M		

132-137

Daimler Fleetline CRL6-30 — Alexander AL — CO43/31F — 1976

132	NFX132P	134	NFX134P	135	NFX135P	136	NFX136P	137	NFX137P
133	NFX133P								

138	VJT138S	Leyland Fleetline FE30ALR	Alexander AL	CO43/31F	1978
139	VJT139S	Leyland Fleetline FE30ALR	Alexander AL	CO43/31F	1978
140	VJT140S	Leyland Fleetline FE30ALR	Alexander AL	CO43/31F	1978

141-160

Leyland Fleetline FE30ALR — Alexander AL — H43/31F — 1978-79

141	AJT141T	145	AJT145T	149	AJT149T	153	ERU153V	157	ERU157V
142	AJT142T	146	AJT146T	150	AJT150T	154	ERU154V	158	ERU158V
143	AJT143T	147	AJT147T	151	ERU151V	155	ERU155V	159	ERU159V
144	AJT144T	148	AJT148T	152	ERU152V	156	ERU156V	160	ERU160V

161-176

Leyland Fleetline FE30AGR — Alexander AL — H43/31F — 1980-81

161	GRU161V	165	GRU165V	168	GRU168V	171	MFX171W	174	MFX174W
162	GRU162V	166	GRU166V	169	MFX169W	172	MFX172W	175	MFX175W
163	GRU163V	167	GRU167V	170	MFX170W	173	MFX173W	176	MFX176W
164	GRU164V								

180-199

Leyland Olympian ONLXB/1R — Marshall — H47/31F* — 1981-82 *183 is DPH47/31F

180	TJT180X	184	TJT184X	188	TJT188X	192	TJT192X	196	TJT196X
181	TJT181X	185	TJT185X	189	TJT189X	193	TJT193X	197	TJT197X
182	TJT182X	186	TJT186X	190	TJT190X	194	TJT194X	198	TJT198X
183	TJT183X	187	TJT187X	191	TJT191X	195	TJT195X	199	TJT199X

200-204

Volvo Citybus B10M-50 — East Lancashire — DPH43/33F 1986

200	D200ELJ	201	C201YPR	202	D202ELJ	203	D203ELJ	204	D204ELJ

205-214

Volvo Citybus B10M-50 — Alexander RH — H47/33F — 1988-89

205	E205GCG	207	E207GCG	209	E209GCG	211	F211WRU	213	F213WRU
206	E206GCG	208	E208GCG	210	F210WRU	212	F212WRU	214	F214WRU

251-269

Dennis Dominator DDA1033 — East Lancashire — H47/33F — 1990-92

251	H251JJT	255	H255JJT	259	H259MFX	264	H264MFX	267	J267SPR
252	H252JJT	256	H256JJT	261	H261MFX	265	H265MFX	268	J268SPR
253	H253JJT	257	H257JJT	262	H262MFX	266	J266SPR	269	J269SPR
254	H254JJT	258	H258MFX	263	H263MFX				

302	D24NWO	Leyland Tiger TRCTL11/3RZ	Duple 320	C48FT	1987	Ex Bebb, Llantwit Fardre, 1989
307	B454AAT	Leyland Tiger TRCTL11/3RH	Plaxton Paramount 3200 II	C50F	1985	Ex East Yorkshire, 1989
333	J333DTS	MAN 16-290	Jonckheere Deauville	C51FT	1992	
336	H815AHS	Volvo B10M-60	Plaxton Paramount 3500 III	C47FT	1991	Ex Park, Hamilton, 1992
337	H818AHS	Volvo B10M-60	Plaxton Paramount 3500 III	C47FT	1991	Ex Park, Hamilton, 1992

338-353

		Volvo B10M-60		Plaxton Expressliner		C49FT*		1990-91	*338/9,344-50 are C46FT	

338	H338KPR	342	G342FFX	345	G345FFX	348	H348JFX	351	H351MLJ
339	H339KPR	343	G343FFX	346	H346JFX	349	H349MLJ	352	H352MLJ
340	J40DTS	344	G344FFX	347	H347JFX	350	J50DTS	353	H353MLJ
341	G341FFX								

Operations:
Dorset Travel Service: 302-353;
Yellow Coaches: 3-9;
Yellow Buses: Remainder

Previous Registrations:

B454AAT	B110WAT, 80EYC	RIB8745	B95TLJ	RIB8748	G981KJX
RIB8743	A993LLJ	RIB8746	B96TLJ	RIB8749	H399MFX
RIB8744	KGS490Y	RIB8747	E646KCX		

Special Liveries:
Overall Advertisements: 183, 191/6.
90th Anniversary livery: 214
National Express: 302/7, 336/7, 340, 351-3
Rapide: 338/9-41-50.

ABUS

OHR184R	Leyland Fleetline FE30AGR	Eastern Coach Works	H43/31F	1977	Ex Thamesdown, 1991	

ARROW COACHES

HNL162N	Leyland National 11351/1R		B52F	1975	Ex Yellow Buses, 1990
JEU571N	Leyland National 11351/1R		B49F	1975	Ex Somerbus, Paulton, 1990
THX211S	Leyland National 10351A/2R		B44F	1978	Ex Thames Transit, 1991
304WPB	Ford R1114	Caetano Estoril	C53F	1978	Ex Barrett, Hanham, 1982
PAE530Y	Mercedes-Benz L307D	Reeve Burgess	C12F	1983	
JYB223Y	Mercedes-Benz L307D	Reeve Burgess	C12F	1983	
A267TAE	Mercedes-Benz L307D	Reeve Burgess	C12F	1984	
A268TAE	Mercedes-Benz L307D	Reeve Burgess	C12F	1984	
59WPG	Scania K112TRS	Jonckheere Jubilee P99	CH51/19CT	1984	Ex NAT, Leeds, 1989
C813KBT	Leyland Cub CU435	Optare	B33F	1985	Ex Sussex Bus, Ford, 1990
D60NOF	Freight Rover Sherpa 365	Carlyle	B18F	1986	Ex Bee Line Buzz, 1990
D240OOJ	Freight Rover Sherpa 365	Carlyle	B18F	1986	Ex Bee Line Buzz, 1990
D262OOJ	Freight Rover Sherpa 365	Carlyle	B18F	1986	Ex Bee Line Buzz, 1990
E402LPR	Bedford YNV	Plaxton Paramount 3200 III	C55F	1987	
E403LPR	Bedford YNV	Plaxton Paramount 3200 III	C55F	1987	
E564UHS	Volvo B10M-61	Plaxton Paramount 3500 III	C53F	1987	Ex Park, Hamilton, 1989
E330OMG	Mercedes-Benz 609D	Reeve Burgess Beaver	B29F	1988	
F936AWW	Volkswagen LT55	Optare City Pacer	DP23F	1988	
F937AWW	Volkswagen LT55	Optare City Pacer	DP23F	1988	
F66SMC	Leyland Swift LBM6T/2RA	Wadham Stringer Vanguard	B39F	1988	
F67SMC	Leyland Swift LBM6T/2RA	Wadham Stringer Vanguard	B39F	1988	
F477PAE	Mercedes-Benz 407D	Made-to-Measure	C16F	1988	
F478PAE	Mercedes-Benz 407D	Made-to-Measure	C16F	1987	
F479PAE	Mercedes-Benz 407D	Made-to-Measure	B16F	1987	
F480PAE	Mercedes-Benz 407D	Made-to-Measure	B17F	1988	
F481PAE	Mercedes-Benz 407D	Made-to-Measure	B16F	1988	
G793UHU	Leyland Swift LBM6T/1RS	Reeve Burgess Harrier	C29F	1989	
G794UHU	Leyland Swift LBM6T/1RS	Reeve Burgess Harrier	C29F	1989	
K576UPG	Mercedes-Benz 609D	Crystals	B20F	1992	

Previous Registrations:

304WPB	XHB559T	59WPG	B505GBD	JEU571N	KNH503N, TVV213

AXE VALLEY

NND961P	Ford Transit 190	Deansgate	C17F	1976	Ex Dodge, London SE16, 1986
FOH370V	Ford Transit 190	Searle	B12C	1980	Acquired 1986
KBL252W	Bedford YNT	Duple Dominant	C53F	1981	Ex Burt, Menheniot, 1992
NPD162W	Ford Transit 190	Dormobile	B16F	1982	Ex Croydon HA, 1988
PYB553Y	Renault-Dodge S56	Rootes	B32F	1984	Ex Woodward, Glossop, 1992
C353BRJ	Volkswagen LT50	Made-to-Measure	C19F	1985	Ex Golynia, Long Melford, 1988
D106TFT	Freight Rover Sherpa 365	Carlyle	B18F	1986	Ex Transcity, Sidcup, 1991
D134LTA	Renault-Dodge S56A	Reeve Burgess	B23F	1986	Ex Plymouth Citybus, 1991
D144LTA	Renault-Dodge S56A	Reeve Burgess	B23F	1986	Ex Plymouth Citybus, 1991
D286RKW	Mercedes-Benz 609D	Reeve Burgess	DP19F	1986	Ex Tellings, Byfleet, 1990

BAKERS

1	E992MHY	Volvo B10M-61	Plaxton Paramount 3500 III	C49F	1988	
2	G823YJF	Volvo B10M-60	Van Hool Alizée	C49FT	1990	
3	F695ONR	Volvo B10M-60	Van Hool Alizée	C49FT	1989	
5	791WHT	Volvo B10M-61	Van Hool Alizée	C53FT	1984	
6	7740KO	Volvo B10M-61	Van Hool Alizée	C49FT	1983	Ex Rowe, Muirkirk, 1986
8	G825YJF	Volvo B10M-60	Van Hool Alizée	C48FT	1990	
9	G824YJF	Volvo B10M-60	Van Hool Alizée	C53FT	1990	
10	612TYB	Volvo B10M-61	Van Hool Alizée H	C49FT	1983	Ex Harris, Armadale, 1986
11	7636LJ	Volvo B10M-61	Van Hool Alizée	C45FT	1983	Ex Harris, Armadale, 1986
12	F421PSE	Dennis Javelin 12SDA1907	Plaxton Paramount 3200 III	C57F	1988	Ex Glennie, New Mills, 1991
14	E761HJF	Dennis Javelin 12SDA1907	Plaxton Paramount 3200 III	C53F	1988	Ex Luckett, Fareham, 1992
15	J858HHU	Dennis Javelin 12SDA1907	Plaxton Paramount 3200 III	C59F	1992	
16	E503JWP	Dennis Javelin 12SDA1908	Plaxton Paramount 3200 III	C57F	1988	Ex Hatts, Foxham, 1992
17	G261JCY	Volvo B10M-60	Plaxton Paramount 3200 III	C53F	1989	
18	F129TRU	Dennis Javelin 12SDA1907	Plaxton Paramount 3200 III	C57F	1988	
19	F131TRU	Dennis Javelin 12SDA1907	Plaxton Paramount 3200 III	C57F	1988	
20	F908UPR	Dennis Javelin 12SDA1907	Plaxton Paramount 3200 III	C57F	1989	
21	G401UOU	Volvo B10M-60	Plaxton Paramount 3200 III	C53F	1989	
22	DHR378V	Bedford YRT	Plaxton Supreme IV	C53F	1980	Ex Leathers, Maiden Bradley, 1988
23	UPV487	Volvo B58-61	Plaxton Supreme IV	C53F	1980	Ex Skyway, Cranleigh, 1983
24	XLH570	Volvo B58-61	Plaxton Supreme IV	C51F	1980	Ex Lewis, Long Ashton, 1983
25	KAU573V	Bedford YMT	Plaxton Supreme IV Exp	C53F	1980	Ex Barton, 1988
26	KAU574V	Bedford YMT	Plaxton Supreme IV Exp	C53F	1980	Ex Barton, 1988
27	KAU575V	Bedford YMT	Plaxton Supreme IV Exp	C53F	1980	Ex Barton, 1988
28	TUA160W	Bedford YMT	Plaxton Supreme IV	C53F	1981	Ex Anderton, Keighley, 1985
29	TUA161W	Bedford YMT	Plaxton Supreme IV	C53F	1981	Ex Anderton, Keighley, 1985
30	299SAE	Volvo B58-61	Plaxton Supreme IV	C57F	1980	
31	HHU31V	Volvo B58-61	Plaxton Supreme IV	C57F	1980	
33	LTY551X	Bedford YNT	Plaxton Supreme V Exp	C53F	1982	Ex Rochester & Marshall, 1990
35	LTY552X	Bedford YNT	Plaxton Supreme V Exp	C53F	1982	Ex Rochester & Marshall, 1990
36	LTY553X	Bedford YNT	Plaxton Supreme V Exp	C53F	1982	Ex Rochester & Marshall, 1990
37	VNT18S	Bedford YLQ	Duple Dominant II	C45F	1978	Ex Herring, Burnham, 1986
39	FTO551V	Bedford YMT	Plaxton Supreme IV Exp	C53F	1980	Ex Barton, 1988
40	OUF359W	Volvo B58-61	Plaxton Supreme IV	C53F	1981	Ex Crawley Luxury, 1991
42	SLH42W	Bedford YMT	Plaxton Supreme IV	C53F	1981	Ex Capital, W Drayton, 1992
43	FTO552V	Bedford YMT	Plaxton Supreme IV Exp	C53F	1980	Ex Barton, 1988
44	SLH43W	Bedford YMT	Plaxton Supreme IV	C53F	1981	Ex Capital, W Drayton, 1992
45	JTM107V	Bedford YMT	Plaxton Supreme IV	C53F	1979	Ex Owen, Knighton, 1985
46	HDV97V	Bedford YMT	Plaxton Supreme IV Exp	C53F	1979	Ex Bow Belle, Crediton, 1985
48	YAA131V	Bedford YMT	Plaxton Supreme IV	C53F	1980	Ex Corinthian, Chandler's Ford, 1985
49	125EWV	Bedford YNT	Van Hool McArdle	C49FT	1982	Ex Meadowcroft, Royton, 1986
50	FTO554V	Bedford YMT	Plaxton Supreme IV Exp	C53F	1979	Ex Barton, 1988
51	LNU578W	Bedford YMT	Plaxton Supreme IV Exp	C53F	1980	Ex Barton, 1988
52	LNU579W	Bedford YMT	Plaxton Supreme IV Exp	C53F	1980	Ex Barton, 1988
53	LNU581W	Bedford YMT	Plaxton Supreme IV Exp	C53F	1980	Ex Barton, 1988
55	YRY1Y	Bedford YMT	Plaxton Supreme IV	C53F	1981	King of the Road, 1991
56	TAY888X	Bedford YMT	Plaxton Supreme IV	C53F	1981	King of the Road, 1991
57	LNU582W	Bedford YMT	Plaxton Supreme IV Exp	C53F	1980	Ex Barton, 1988
58	XPO829V	Bedford YMT	Plaxton Supreme IV	C53F	1980	Ex Luckett, Wallington, 1986
60	F369CHE	Scania K113TRB	Plaxton Paramount 4000 III	CH38/16CT	1988	
61	C342GSD	Volvo B10MT-53	Van Hool Astromega	CH47/25CT	1985	
62	C861MGB	Scania K112TRB	Plaxton Paramount 4000 III	CH55/16CT	1986	Ex Western Scottish, 1991
63	E331PWO	Scania K112TRS	Plaxton Paramount 4000 II	CH55/18CT	1987	Ex Thomas, Clydach Vale, 1992
64	WTU495W	Bristol VRT/SL3/501(6LXB)	Eastern Coach Works	H43/31F	1981	Ex Crosville Wales, 1991
65	JOV686P	Bristol VRT/SL2/6LX	MCW	H43/33F	1975	Ex West Midlands, 1986

66	JOV709P	Bristol VRT/SL2/6LX	MCW	H43/33F	1975	Ex West Midlands, 1986
67	UGR694R	Bristol VRT/SL3/6LXB	Eastern Coach Works	H43/31F	1976	Ex Northumbria, 1989
68	UGR695R	Bristol VRT/SL3/6LXB	Eastern Coach Works	H43/31F	1976	Ex Northumbria, 1989
69	PKE805M	Bristol VRT/SL2/6LX	Eastern Coach Works	H43/34F	1973	Ex Berry, Taunton, 1992
70	E521TOV	Iveco Daily 49.10	Carlyle Dailybus	B25F	1988	
71	E522TOV	Iveco Daily 49.10	Carlyle Dailybus	B25F	1988	
72	E694UND	Mercedes-Benz 609D	Made-to-Measure	B21F	1988	Ex A-Line, Felling, 1990
73	C432VGX	Mercedes-Benz L608D	Rootes	C19F	1985	Ex Crystals, Dartford, 1990
74	B91WPX	Mercedes-Benz L608D	Robin Hood	C21F	1984	Ex Smith, Buntingford, 1991
80	VBC984X	Bedford YMT	Plaxton Supreme IV	C53F	1982	Ex Mountford, Manchester, 1992
83	315MWL	Bedford YMT	Plaxton Supreme IV	C53F	1980	Ex Barnes, Puriton, 1991
85	6108BT	Bedford YNT	Plaxton Supreme IV	C38FT	1982	Ex Palmer, Dunstable, 1992
87	XEL542X	Bedford YNT	Plaxton Supreme IV	C53F	1982	Ex Beeline, Warminster, 1992
87A	VNK475M	Bedford YRT	Duple Dominant	C53F	1974	Ex Barnes, Puriton, 1991
88	LHW506P	Bedford YMT	Plaxton Supreme III	C53F	1976	Ex Barnes, Puriton, 1991
89	BCU23V	Bedford YMT	Plaxton Supreme IV Exp	C53F	1980	Ex Wansbeck, Ashington, 1985

Previous Registrations:

125EWV	BLU740X	7636LJ	LYS512Y	HHU31V	BEU817V, 340MYA
299SAE	BEU816V	7740KO	USD224Y	OUF359W	FTH991W, 789CLC
315MWL	DKG271Y	791WHT	A767UHT	UPV487	HPL422V
340MYA	??	958VKM	VJY921V	XEL842X	WFX74X, YBK605
6108BT	DNK107Y	C432VGX	C390CKK, CSV907	XHT48T	DYA979T, 612TYB
612TYB	NDS835Y	C861MGB	C352DWR, VLT37	XLH570	GPL522V

BEELINE (Warminster)

WRR365M	Bedford YRT	Duple Dominant	C53F	1973	Ex Barton, 1981
528JOP	Bedford YRT	Wright Contour (1984)	C53F	1974	Ex Earnside, Glenfarg, 1978
YVO300M	Bedford YRT	Duple Dominant	C53F	1974	Ex Thomsett, Deal, 1991
KYA99N	Bedford YRT	Duple Dominant	C53F	1975	Ex Winford Queen, 1986
LNM901P	Bedford YRT	Duple Dominant	C53F	1976	Ex Alpha, Brighton, 1989
NWK5P	Bedford YMT	Plaxton Supreme III	C53F	1976	Ex Victoria Tours, Handley, 1989
UHL218S	Bedford YMT	Duple Dominant	C53F	1978	Ex Globe, Barnsley, 1981
500KUO	Bedford YMT	Van Hool McArdle	C53F	1978	Ex Ridler, Dulverton, 1990
WKE67S	Bedford YMT	Duple Dominant	B61F	1978	Ex Metrowest, Oldfield, 1990
MCG642T	Bedford YMT	Duple Dominant II	C53F	1978	
CWA439T	Bedford YMT	Duple Dominant	B55F	1979	Ex Northern, North Anston, 1989
XPL889T	Bedford YMT	Duple Dominant	B61F	1979	Ex Boro'line, 1991
YAM870T	Bedford YLQ	Duple Dominant	B53F	1979	Ex Perry, Bromyard, 1990
LNU577W	Bedford YMT	Plaxton Supreme IV Exp	C53F	1980	Ex Morris, Llanfyllin, 1991
MJU3W	Bedford YMT	Plaxton Supreme IV	C53F	1980	Ex White, Huthwaite, 1990
UPB668X	Bedford YNT	Plaxton Supreme V	C53F	1982	Ex Lever, East Knoyle, 1991
XEL542X	Bedford YNT	Plaxton Supreme V	C53F	1982	Ex Lever, East Knoyle, 1991
OEU209V	Mercedes-Benz L608D	Reeve Burgess	C21F	1983	Ex Clapton Coaches, 1991
DSV782	Bedford YNT	Plaxton Paramount 3200 II	C53F	1986	
DSV783	Bedford YNT	Plaxton Paramount 3200 II	C53F	1986	

Previous Registrations:

500KUO	TOH733S	DSV782	From new	XEL542X	WFX74X, YBK605
528JOP	SKG811M	DSV783	From new	YAM870T	WBX2T, WNT244

BERE REGIS

GRP922N	Bedford YRQ	Willowbrook	B45F	1974	Ex United Counties, 1984
JFX232N	Bedford YRT	Plaxton Elite III	DP53F	1975	
JFX233N	Bedford YRT	Plaxton Elite III	DP53F	1975	
JFX234N	Bedford YRT	Plaxton Elite III	DP53F	1975	
JFX235N	Bedford YRT	Plaxton Elite III	DP53F	1975	

	Bedford YMT	Plaxton Supreme III	C53F	1977	962/3 ex Sonner, Gillingham, 1981
RLJ186R	RLJ188R	SFX785R		VMJ962S	VMJ963S
RLJ187R	SFX784R				

UFX330	Volvo B58-61	Duple Dominant II	C53F	1980	Ex Shearings, 1987

	Volvo B58-61	Duple Dominant II	C57F	1980	Ex Shearings, 1987
HJP482V	HJP484V	HJP485V	HJP487V		HJP488V
HJP483V					

	Volvo B10M-61	Duple Dominant IV	C53F	1983	Ex Shearings, 1989
ENF560Y	ENF561Y	ENF564Y	ENF568Y		ENF573Y

A287LNF	Ford Transit 190	Dixon Lomas	DP16F	1984	
A531MVU	Ford Transit 190	Dixon Lomas	DP16F	1984	
A599LJT	Volvo B10M-61	Duple Caribbean	C55F	1984	
A600LJT	Volvo B10M-61	Duple Caribbean	C55F	1984	
OJT568	Volvo B10M-61	Plaxton Paramount 3200 II	C57F	1986	
UFX567	Volvo B10M-61	Duple 340	C55F	1986	
901CDU	Volvo B10M-46	Plaxton Paramount 3200 II	C39F	1987	
E217GCG	Volvo B10M-61	Plaxton Paramount 3500 III	C53F	1988	
E218GCG	Volvo B10M-61	Plaxton Paramount 3500 III	C53F	1988	
E219GCG	Volvo B10M-61	Plaxton Paramount 3500 III	C53F	1988	

	Volvo B10M-61	Ikarus Blue Danube	C53F	1988	
E220GCG	E221GCG	E222GCG	E223GCG		E224GCG

G432SNN	Volvo B10M-60	Ikarus Blue Danube	C53F	1989	
UXF850	Volvo B10M-60	Ikarus Blue Danube	C53F	1989	Ex Arena, Liverpool, 1991
H443JLJ	Volvo B10M-60	Plaxton Paramount 3200 III	C57F	1990	

Previous Registrations:

901CDU	From new	UFX330	HJP498V	UXF850	G734TJF
OJT568	From new	UFX567	From new		

BERRY'S

KYB285K	Bedford YRQ	Plaxton Elite II	C45F	1972	
MYD599L	AEC Reliance 6U3ZR	Plaxton Elite III	C51F	1973	
WGN828M	AEC Reliance 6U3ZR	Plaxton Elite III	C51F	1974	Ex Surrey Motors, Sutton, 1980
JYA941N	Bedford YRQ	Plaxton Elite III	C45F	1975	
PYA646P	AEC Reliance 6U3ZR	Plaxton Elite III	C51F	1976	
UGP97R	AEC Reliance 6U3ZR	Plaxton Supreme III	C51F	1976	Ex Surrey Motors, Sutton, 1980
UYC860R	Bedford YLQ	Plaxton Supreme III	C45F	1977	
AYA912S	Bedford YLQ	Plaxton Supreme III	C45F	1978	
XAN48T	Bristol VRT/SL3/6LXB	Eastern Coach Works	H43/34F	1978	Ex Roselyn, Par, 1990
XAN431T	Bristol VRT/SL3/6LXB	Eastern Coach Works	H43/34F	1978	Ex Roselyn, Par, 1991
AJH854T	Bristol VRT/SL3/6LXB	Eastern Coach Works	H41/34F	1979	Ex Eagle, Bristol, 1991
AJH855T	Bristol VRT/SL3/6LXB	Eastern Coach Works	H41/34F	1979	Ex Eagle, Bristol, 1991
PIB2470	Volvo B10M-61	Jonckheere Bermuda	C49FT	1982	Ex Volvo Bus, 1982
PIB3360	Volvo B10M-61	Van Hool Alizée	C46FT	1983	Ex Volvo Bus, 1983
PIB5767	Volvo B10M-61	Van Hool Alizée	C49FT	1983	
B100CCS	Volvo B10M-61	Jonckheere Jubilee P50	C48FT	1984	Ex Volvo Bus, 1985
B910SPR	Volvo B10M-61	Plaxton Paramount 3200 II	C53F	1985	Ex Excelsior, Bournemouth, 1987
C308FYA	Volvo B10M-53	Plaxton Paramount 4000	CH53/9F	1985	
C785HYA	Volvo B10M-61	Jonckheere Jubilee P599	C51FT	1986	
C786HYA	Volvo B10M-61	Jonckheere Jubilee P599	C51FT	1986	
D260HFX	Volvo B10M-61	Plaxton Paramount 3200 III	C53F	1986	Ex Excelsior, Bournemouth, 1989
D547OYD	Volvo B10M-61	Van Hool Alizée	C49FT	1987	
E677VDA	Volvo B10M-53	Plaxton Paramount 4000 II	CH54/11CT	1987	Ex Flights, Birmingham, 1990
E63XYC	Volvo B10M-61	Van Hool Alizée	C49FT	1988	
E22XYD	Volvo B10M-53	Van Hool Astron	CH51/13DT	1988	
F121GYB	Volvo B10M-60	Van Hool Alizée	C49FT	1989	
F476WFX	Volvo B10M-60	Plaxton Paramount 3200 III	C53F	1989	Ex Excelsior, Bournemouth, 1989
G846NYC	Volvo B10M-60	Jonckheere Deauville	C51FT	1990	
J819EYC	Volvo B10M-60	Jonckheere Deauville	C51F	1992	
K	Volvo B12T-60	Van Hool Astrobel	CH51/13DT	On order	

Special Liveries: Beaverbus: AJH854/5T, XAN48/431T

Previous Registrations:

PIB2470	CNS563X	PIB3360	RSJ826Y	PIB5767	JYC794Y

BLANDFORD BUS COMPANY

7682LJ	Bristol Lodekka FL6G	Eastern Coach Works	H37/33RD	1962	Ex driver trainer, 1990
NHB190M	Bristol RESL6G	Eastern Coach Works	B47F	1973	Ex Pennine Blue, Denton, 1992
GCL349N	Bristol RELH6G	Eastern Coach Works	DP49F	1974	Ex Catch A Bus, East Bolden, 1992
FDV786V	Bristol LHS6L	Eastern Coach Works	B35F	1979	Ex Western National, 1992
FBV272W	Bristol LHS6L	Eastern Coach Works	B35F	1980	Ex Bluebird Northern, 1992
KDL204W	Bristol LHS6L	Eastern Coach Works	DP31F	1980	Ex Solent Blue Line, 1990
5684EL	Toyota Coaster BB30R	Caetano Optimo	C19F	1986	Ex Smith, Rugby, 1990

Previous Registrations: 5684EL   7930EL

BROOKSIDE TRAVEL

HJT39N	Bristol LH6L	Eastern Coach Works	B43F	1973	Ex Teesside, Stockton, 1991
TCV646N	Leyland Leopard PSU3E/4R	Plaxton Supreme III	C53F	1978	Ex Compass Bus, Wakefield, 1992
OO1961	AEC Reliance 6U2R	Plaxton Supreme III Exp	C53F	1978	Ex Filer, Stanton Wick, 1989
CTM400T	Bedford VAS5	Plaxton Supreme	C29F	1979	Ex Booth, Eccles, 1988
MFE391V	Bedford YLQ	Plaxton Supreme IV	C45F	1980	Ex Hornsby, Ashby, 1988
GBB254	Bedford YNT	Plaxton Supreme VI Exp	C49F	1982	Ex Go-Whittle, 1992
B400RHN	Ford Transit 190	Carlyle	B16F	1984	Ex United, 1990
D741JUB	Freight Rover Sherpa 350D	Carlyle	B16F	1987	Ex Barry, Liskeard, 1991
D128LTA	Renault-Dodge S56	Reeve Burgess Beaver	B23F	1986	Ex Plymouth, 1991
D150LTA	Renault-Dodge S56	Reeve Burgess Beaver	B23F	1986	Ex Plymouth, 1992
D173LTA	Renault-Dodge S56	Reeve Burgess Beaver	B23F	1987	Ex Plymouth, 1991
D174LTA	Renault-Dodge S56	Reeve Burgess Beaver	B23F	1987	Ex Plymouth, 1992

Previous Registrations:
GBB254   PNT850X   OO1961   VPH35S   TCV646N   UWE89S, GUN162

CASTLEWAYS

EDG250L	Leyland Leopard PSU3B/4R	Plaxton Elite III Exp	C49F	1972	
FAD708T	Bedford YMT	Plaxton Supreme IV Exp	C49F	1979	
LFH719V	Leyland Leopard PSU3E/4R	Plaxton Supreme IV Exp	C49F	1980	
LFH720V	Leyland Leopard PSU3E/4R	Plaxton Supreme IV Exp	C49F	1980	
CFH747Y	Mercedes-Benz L307D	Devon Conversions	C12F	1983	Ex Crabtree, Brockworth, 1985
TJF757	Van Hool T815H	Van Hool Alicron	C49FT	1986	
E130NFH	Kässbohrer Setra S215HR	Kässbohrer Rational	C53F	1988	
86JBF	Van Hool T815H	Van Hool Alicron	C49FT	1990	
H383HFH	Mercedes-Benz 814D	Reeve Burgess Beaver	DP33F	1991	
J306KFP	Toyota HB31R	Caetano Optimo	C21F	1991	
J362BNW	Mercedes-Benz 811D	Optare StarRider	DP29F	1991	
J688MFE	Kässbohrer Setra S215HR	Kässbohrer Rational	C53F	1992	
J689MFE	Kässbohrer Setra S215HR	Kässbohrer Rational	C53F	1992	

Previous Registrations: 86JBF   G901ANR   TJF757   From new

CIRCLE-LINE

WRP767J	Bristol VRT/SL6G	Eastern Coach Works	H39/31F	1970	Ex Applegates, Berkeley, 1991
GVH147L	Daimler Fleetline CRG6LX	Roe	H45/29D	1972	Ex Yorkshire Rider, 1987
XTF818L	Leyland Leopard PSU3B/4R	Duple Dominant	C53F	1973	Ex Ribble, 1987
ETO162L	Daimler Fleetline CRG6LX	Willowbrook	H44/34D	1973	Ex Nottingham, 1985
ETO164L	Daimler Fleetline CRG6LX	Willowbrook	H44/34D	1973	Ex Nottingham, 1985
TRT97M	Leyland Atlantean AN68/1R	Roe	H43/29D	1973	Ex Eastbourne, 1990
NFA12M	Daimler Fleetline CRG6LX	Willowbrook	H44/33F	1974	Ex Stevenson, Spath, 1986
NFA15M	Daimler Fleetline CRG6LX	Willowbrook	H44/33F	1974	Ex Stevenson, Spath, 1986
THM662M	Daimler Fleetline CRL6	MCW	H44/24D	1974	Ex Stevenson, Spath, 1985
KKW65P	Leyland Leopard PSU3C/4R	Alexander AY	DP19DL	1976	Ex South Yorkshire, 1990
MWJ466P	Leyland Leopard PSU3C/4R	Duple Dominant	C53F	1976	Ex Eastbourne, 1989
MWJ471P	Leyland Leopard PSU3C/4R	Duple Dominant	C53F	1976	Ex Eastbourne, 1989
LEU261P	Bristol VRT/SL3/6LXB	Eastern Coach Works	H43/27D	1976	Ex Badgerline, 1991
LEU266P	Bristol VRT/SL3/6LXB	Eastern Coach Works	H43/27D	1976	Ex City Line, 1990
LEU267P	Bristol VRT/SL3/6LXB	Eastern Coach Works	H43/27D	1976	Ex City Line, 1990

KUC220P	Daimler Fleetline CRL6	MCW	CO44/34F	1976	Ex Stevenson, Spath, 1989
OJD187R	Leyland Fleetline FE30AGR	MCW	H44/24D	1977	Ex Stevenson, Spath, 1988
OJD199R	Leyland Fleetline FE30AGR	MCW	H43/33F	1977	Ex Norfolks, Nayland, 1990
OJD208R	Leyland Fleetline FE30AGR	MCW	H44/24D	1977	Ex Stevenson, Spath, 1988
PPH468R	Bristol VRT/SL3/501(6LXB)	Eastern Coach Works	H43/31F	1977	Ex Swanbrook, 1991
PHY693S	Bristol VRT/SL3/6LXB	Eastern Coach Works	H43/27D	1977	Ex City Line, 1990
ASD841T	Seddon Pennine 7	Alexander AY	B53F	1979	Ex Stevenson, Spath, 1992
BSD848T	Seddon Pennine 7	Alexander AY	B53F	1979	Ex Stevenson, Spath, 1992
XSD604T	Seddon Pennine 7	Alexander AY	DP49F	1979	Ex Western Scottish, 1992
XSD607T	Seddon Pennine 7	Alexander AY	DP49F	1979	Ex Western Scottish, 1992
SSX598V	Seddon Pennine 7	Alexander AYS	B53F	1980	Ex Stevenson, Spath, 1992
C693VAD	Leyland Cub CU435/4R	Wadham Stringer Vanguard	B32FL	1986	Ex Gloucester CC, 1992
C694VAD	Leyland Cub CU435/4R	Wadham Stringer Vanguard	B32FL	1986	Ex Gloucester CC, 1992
C696VAD	Leyland Cub CU435/4R	Wadham Stringer Vanguard	B32FL	1986	Ex Gloucester CC, 1992
C697VAD	Leyland Cub CU435/4R	Wadham Stringer Vanguard	B32FL	1986	Ex Gloucester CC, 1992
D604HTC	Iveco 79.14	Robin Hood	B30FL	1987	Ex Gloucester CC, 1992
D605HTC	Iveco 79.14	Robin Hood	B30FL	1987	Ex Gloucester CC, 1992
E638MMS	Ford Transit VE6	Ford	B14F	1987	Ex Ivory, Armley, 1992

Special Liveries:
Cheltenham Town Service: ASD841T.
Overall Advertisements: GVH147L, ETO162L, NFA12/5M, KUC220P, OJD208R

CLAPTON COACHES

PIJ660	Leyland Leopard PSU3E/4R	Willowbrook Warrior (1992)	B48F	1978	Ex PMT, 1992
DSK660	Leyland Leopard PSU3E/4R	Willowbrook Warrior (1992)	B48F	1978	Ex Kinch, Leicester, 1992
B374WHY	Mercedes-Benz L307D	Imperial	C12F	1985	
E900VMW	Mercedes-Benz L307D	Reeve Burgess	C12F	1987	
E930YAM	Mercedes-Benz 507D	Reeve Burgess	DP16F	1988	
E350AMR	Mercedes-Benz 609D	Reeve Burgess Beaver	DP25F	1988	
E971NMK	Mercedes-Benz 609D	Reeve Burgess Beaver	DP25F	1988	Ex Dines Way, Boreham, 1990
F850TCW	Mercedes-Benz 609D	Reeve Burgess Beaver	B20F	1988	
F695AWW	Mercedes-Benz 811D	Optare StarRider	B33F	1988	Ex Dobson, Lostock Gralam, 1991
VDJ660	Bova FHD12/290	Bova Futura	C51FT	1988	Ex Cross Keys, Newingreen, 1989
F165XCS	Mercedes-Benz 609D	Scott	C24F	1989	Ex Clyde Coast, Ardrossan, 1990
KSK660	Bova FHD12/290	Bova Futura	C55F	1989	Ex Avalon, Glastonbury, 1992
660FHU	Bova FHD12/290	Bova Futura	C49FT	1990	
J850OBV	Mercedes-Benz 709D	Reeve Burgess Beaver	B23F	1992	

Previous Registrations:
660FHU	From new		KSK660	F690FYC	VDJ660	F26EKR
DSK660	VRM620S		PIJ660	XBF60S		

COTTRELL'S

EAD122T	Leyland Fleetline FE33ALR	Northern Counties	H47/36F	1979	
GBU2V	MCW Metrobus DR101/6	MCW	H43/30F	1979	Ex Greater Manchester, 1986
GBU6V	MCW Metrobus DR101/6	MCW	H43/30F	1979	Ex Greater Manchester, 1986
GDF332V	Volvo B58-56	Plaxton Supreme IV	C51F	1979	
MNM33V	Leyland Leopard PSU3E/4R	Plaxton Supreme IV Exp	C53F	1980	Ex British Airways, 1983
PAD806W	Leyland Leopard PSU3E/4R	Plaxton Supreme IV Exp	C51F	1981	
XPP286X	Leyland Tiger TRCTL11/3R	Plaxton Supreme V	C57F	1981	Ex Tri-Star, West Drayton, 1986
VUD149X	Leyland Tiger TRCTL11/3R	Plaxton Supreme V Exp	C53F	1982	Ex Harrod, Wormegay, 1987
KBM14Y	Leyland Tiger TRCTL11/3R	Plaxton Paramount 3200	C57F	1983	Ex Premier, St Albans, 1987
NDE147Y	Leyland Tiger TRCTL11/2R	Plaxton Paramount 3200 E	C53F	1983	Ex Horlock, Northfleet, 1988
C474CAP	Leyland Tiger TRCTL11/3RH	Plaxton Paramount 3200 II	C51F	1986	Ex Thames Transit, 1991
D803NBO	Leyland Tiger TRCTL11/3RH	Plaxton Paramount 3500 II	C51FT	1987	Ex Merthyr Tydfil, 1989
E688UNE	Leyland Tiger TRCTL11/3RZ	Plaxton Paramount 3200 III	C53F	1988	Ex Shearings, 1992
F183UFH	Leyland Tiger TRCTL11/3RZM	Plaxton Paramount 3200 III	C55F	1989	

CROWN

GRS118E	Leyland Atlantean PDR1/1	Alexander A	H44/34F	1967	Ex Watson, Whyteleafe, 1992
NDR509J	Leyland Atlantean PDR2/1	Park Royal	H47/30D	1971	Ex Mr Video, Torquay, 1992

PPH465R	Bristol VRT/SL3/501(6LXB)	Eastern Coach Works	H43/31F	1977	Ex Badgerline, 1987
PPH471R	Bristol VRT/SL3/501(6LXB)	Eastern Coach Works	H43/31F	1977	Ex Badgerline, 1987
PPH472R	Bristol VRT/SL3/501(6LXB)	Eastern Coach Works	H43/31F	1977	Ex Badgerline, 1987
PPH474R	Bristol VRT/SL3/501	Eastern Coach Works	H43/31F	1977	Ex Badgerline, 1987
366XHY	Leyland Leopard PSU3E/4R	Plaxton Supreme IV	C44FT	1979	
ULS646T	Leyland Leopard PSU3E/4R	Duple Dominant	C49F	1979	Ex Filer's, Ilfracombe, 1992
WTH480T	Leyland Leopard PSU3E/4RT	Duple Dominant	C49F	1979	Ex Badgerline, 1992
LUE240V	Ford R1114	Plaxton Supreme IV Exp	C53F	1980	Ex Allenways, Birmingham, 1986
LJU905V	Ford R1114	Plaxton Supreme IV	C53F	1980	Ex Stevenson, Spath, 1988
FTC2W	Leyland Leopard PSU3/4R	Plaxton Supreme IV (1981)	C49F	1965	Ex Greenslades, Exeter, 1977
FTC3W	Leyland Leopard PSU3/4R	Plaxton Supreme IV (1981)	C51F	1964	Ex Hills, Tredegar, 1972
RJU383W	Ford R1114	Plaxton Supreme IV	C53F	1981	Ex Stevenson, Spath, 1988
BDF205Y	Leyland Tiger TRCTL11/3R	Eastern Coach Works	C51F	1983	Ex Wessex, Bristol, 1992
A329XHE	Leyland Royal Tiger B50	Plaxton Paramount 3500	C47FT	1984	Ex West Riding, 1988
B298AMG	Leyland Royal Tiger B50	Plaxton Paramount 3500	C53F	1984	Ex Trina, London WC2, 1987
C496BFB	Ford Transit 190	Dormobile	B16F	1985	Ex Badgerline, 1992
D204KWT	Freight Rover Sherpa 374	Dormobile	B16F	1986	Ex West Riding, 1988
D841LND	Renault-Dodge S56	Northern Counties	B20F	1986	Ex GM Buses, 1992
D801NBO	Leyland Royal Tiger B50	Leyland	C49FT	1986	Ex Merthyr Tydfil, 1989
D802NBO	Leyland Tiger TRCTL11/3RH	Plaxton Paramount 3500 II	C53F	1986	Ex Merthyr Tydfil, 1989
D283XCX	DAF SB2305DHTD585	Plaxton Paramount 3200	C53F	1987	Ex Bennett, Gloucester, 1992
E211JDD	DAF SB2305DHTD585	Plaxton Paramount 3200	C53F	1987	Ex Bennett, Gloucester, 1992
G783UHY	Leyland DAF Sherpa 400	Leyland DAF	B16F	1989	

Previous Registrations:

366XHY	VHW266T	FTC3W	8757HA
FTC2W	CHA94C	LJU905V	LJF735V, OFA10

DAWLISH COACHES

TSV850	AEC Reliance 2MU3RA	Harrington Cavalier	C40F	1964	Ex Allmey, Eastcote, 1985
TGX755M	Daimler Fleetline CRL6	Park Royal	H44/28D	1974	Ex Crown Coaches, Bristol, 1990
MVY543P	Daimler Fleetline CRG6LX	Roe	H44/34F	1975	Ex York Pullman, 1985
FDN583S	Leyland Fleetline FE30AGR	Roe	H45/35F	1978	Ex York Pullman, 1985
CKH454X	Mercedes-Benz L608D	Plaxton Mini Supreme	C25F	1982	Ex Wallace Arnold, 1989
FIL7283	DAF MB200DKFL600	Van Hool Alizée	C49FT	1983	
710HTA	Volvo B10M-61	Van Hool Alizée	C49FT	1983	Ex Ford, Gunnislake, 1987
8RDV	Volvo B10M-61	Van Hool Alizée	C49FT	1984	
A168PAE	Volvo B10M-61	Duple Laser	C57F	1984	Ex Turner, Bristol, 1992
A169PAE	Volvo B10M-61	Duple Laser	C57F	1984	Ex Turner, Bristol, 1992
D127ACX	DAF MB230DKFL615	Plaxton Paramount 3500 III	C53F	1987	Ex Park, Hamilton, 1987
D630YCX	DAF MB230DKFL615	Plaxton Paramount 3500 III	C53F	1987	Ex Park, Hamilton, 1987
E181BTT	Mercedes-Benz 609D	Devon Conversions	C23F	1988	
E592EHS	Volvo B10M-61	Plaxton Paramount 3500 III	C53FT	1988	Ex Arkle Travel, Torquay, 1991
E296OMG	Volvo B10M-61	Van Hool Alizée	C49FT	1988	Ex North Mymms, Potters Bar, 1991
F276WAF	Volvo B10M-61	Van Hool Alizée	C49FT	1989	Ex Ford, Gunnislake, 1990
F994HGE	Volvo B10M-60	Plaxton Paramount 3500 III	C49FT	1989	Ex Park, Hamilton, 1990
F59JTA	DAF SB3000DKV601	Caetano Algarve	C49FT	1989	Ex Arkle Travel, Torquay, 1990
F512LTT	Volvo B10M-60	Van Hool Alizée	C49FT	1989	
F77MFJ	Volvo B10M-60	Van Hool Alizée	C53F	1989	
F459NDV	Dennis Javelin 12SDA1907	Plaxton Paramount 3200 III	C53F	1989	
F427XCV	Mercedes-Benz 811D	Robin Hood	C25F	1989	Ex Pollard, Ruan Minor, 1990
G40HKY	MCW MetroRider MF154/2	MCW	C28F	1990	Ex Neighbour, High Wycombe, 1992

Previous Registrations:

710HTA	TCV138Y	A168PAE	A879UHY, 3138DP	FIL7283	GFJ820Y
8RDV	A896PTA	A169PAE	A880UHY, 2170MV	TSV850	4RDV

Special Liveries:
Majestic Holidays: FIL7284, D127ACX, D630YCX, F77MFJ, F459NDV

DEVON SERVICES

TBU740G	Bristol LH6L	Plaxton Panorama Elite	DP45F	1969	Ex Perry, Bromyard, 1990
EPY315L	Ford R192	Willowbrook	B44F	1973	Ex Devonways, Totnes, 1989
LNK787L	Leyland Leopard PSU5/4R	Plaxton Elite III	C57F	1973	Ex Truronian, Truro, 1989
RPH111L	Bristol LHS6L	Eastern Coach Works	B37F	1973	Ex Nightingale, Exmouth, 1990

VLF209M	Leyland Leopard PSU5/4R	Duple Dominant	C57F	1974	Ex Tellyn, Witham, 1987
BNE767N	Bristol LH6L	Eastern Coach Works	B43F	1974	Ex Teesside MS, 1990
GPD316N	Bristol LHS6L	Eastern Coach Works	DP35F	1974	Ex Greenslades, Exeter, 1990
RTT420N	Bristol RELH6L	Plaxton Elite III	C51F	1974	Ex Goodridge, Rawmarsh, 1990
GLS278N	Leyland Leopard PSU3/3R	Alexander AYS	B53F	1974	Ex Layland, Paignton, 1989
OJD17R	Bristol LHS6L	Eastern Coach Works	B26F	1976	Ex Linkfast, Hadleigh, 1990
SFJ112R	Bristol LH6L	Plaxton Supreme III Exp	C43F	1977	Ex Tally Ho!, Kingsbridge, 1990
UFH277	Leyland Leopard PSU5A/4R	Plaxton Supreme III Exp	C53F	1977	Ex Waddell, Lochwinnoch, 1989
IIJ145	Leyland Leopard PSU3C/4R	Plaxton Viewmaster	C49F	1978	Ex Devonways, Totnes, 1990
HIL7983	Volvo B58-61	Duple Dominant II	C48FT	1978	Ex Devonways, Totnes, 1990
GPA610V	Volvo B58-61	Plaxton Supreme IV	C49DL	1978	Ex Cole, Crayford, 1992
FPN996V	Bedford YMT	Unicar	C53F	1979	Ex Heward, Torquay, 1991
HIL7563	Leyland Tiger TRCTL11/3R	Plaxton Viewmaster IV	C49FT	1982	Ex Fairley, Spennymoor, 1992

Previous Registrations:

EPY315L	J30452	IIJ145	SOJ702S
HIL7563	AUA351X, 668HCG, OVN686X	UFH277	SUR280R, 190CUD, WGD971R
HIL7983	GPA610V		

DUKE'S TRAVEL

676GBD	Leyland Leopard PSU3B/4R	Plaxton Elite II	C53F	1971	Ex Nash, Milkwall, 1985
862EHT	Leyland Leopard PSU5A/4R	Plaxton Supreme III	C55F	1977	Ex Lever, East Knoyle, 1987
CYC329A	Leyland Leopard PSU3E/4R	Plaxton Supreme III	C53F	1977	Ex Hughes, Llanfair, 1989
AEF878A	Leyland Leopard PSU3E/4R	Plaxton Viewmaster IV	C53F	1979	Ex Fitzjohn, Bournemouth, 1990
TAD24W	Leyland Tiger TRCTL11/3R	Plaxton Supreme IV	C50F	1981	Ex Warner, Tewkesbury, 1991
MYO486X	Leyland Leopard PSU5C/4R	Wadham Stringer Vanguard	B52F	1981	Ex MoD, 1991
PAT189W	Leyland Royal Tiger B50	Roe Doyen	C47FT	1984	Ex Warner, Tewkesbury, 1991
116XYD	Leyland Tiger TRCTL11/3R	Plaxton Paramount 3500	C53FT	1984	Ex Lewis, London SE10, 1988
C496BFB	Ford Transit 190	Dormobile	B16F	1986	Ex Badgerline, 1992
666VHU	Leyland Tiger TRCTL11/3R	Van Hool Alizée	C49FT	1987	Ex Tellings-Golden Miller, 1992

Previous Registrations:

116XYD	A614HGY	862EHT	WGK333R		PAT189W	A101GAD, 3012WF
666VHU	OKY85R	AEF878A	JTM104V		TAD24W	SDG25W, 4529WF
676GBD	CUA583J	CYC329A	STV16R			

DURBIN

HTC726N	Bristol VRT/SL2/6LXB	Eastern Coach Works	H39/31F	1975	Ex Badgerline, 1992
LEU262P	Bristol VRT/SL3/6LXB	Eastern Coach Works	H43/27D	1976	Ex Teagle, Bristol, 1991
NBD101P	Bedford YRT	Caetano Estoril	C53F	1976	Ex Reid, Patchway, 1985
GCX61S	Ford R1114	Caetano Estoril	C53F	1978	Ex Woodspring, Portishead, 1989
URF668S	Bristol VRT/SL3/501	Eastern Coach Works	H43/31F	1978	Ex PMT, 1992
WKO131S	Bristol VRT/SL3/6LXB	Eastern Coach Works	H43/31F	1978	Ex Maidstone & District, 1992
YEU342V	Ford R1014	Plaxton Supreme IV Exp	C45F	1979	Ex Woodspring, Portishead, 1989
CVJ505V	Bedford CFL	Dormobile	B12F	1979	Ex Woodspring, Portishead, 1989
LPP349V	Ford R1014	Duple Dominant II	C29F	1979	Ex Mott, Stoke Mandeville, 1990
KPP621V	Ford R1014	Duple Dominant II	C45F	1980	Ex Radford, Chichester, 1991
HVU521V	Ford R1114	Duple Dominant II	C53F	1980	Ex Axe Vale, Biddisham, 1989
DFB672W	Leyland Leopard PSU5D/4R	Duple Dominant II	C57F	1981	Ex Collis, Bristol, 1988
EHU750W	Ford R1115	Duple Dominant IV	C53F	1981	Ex Stevens, Bristol, 1991
EHU751W	Ford R1115	Duple Dominant IV	C53F	1981	Ex Avon CC, 1989
LFR278X	Fiat 60F10	Harwin	B20F	1982	Ex Crown, Bristol, 1991
UWA580Y	Ford R1114	Duple Dominant IV	C53F	1983	Ex Avon CC, 1989
FWH39Y	Leyland Tiger TRCTL11/3R	Plaxton Paramount 3500	C49F	1983	Ex Canavan, Kilsyth, 1991
A105EBC	Ford R1115	Plaxton Paramount 3200	C53F	1984	Ex Glenvic, Bristol, 1991
A455JJF	DAF MB200DKFL600	Duple Caribbean	C55F	1984	Ex Eastville, Bristol, 1992
A985UFB	DAF MB200DKTL600	Plaxton Paramount 3500	C51F	1984	Ex Maidstone & District, 1992
A611XKU	Leyland Tiger TRCTL11/3R	Plaxton Paramount 3200	C57F	1983	Ex Godson, Leeds, 1992
C305AHP	DAF SB2300DHS585	Duple 340	C57F	1986	Ex Travelfar, Henfield, 1991
D390JBA	Freight Rover Sherpa 350	Freight Rover	B16F	1986	Acquired 1989
D760JUB	Freight Rover Sherpa 374	Dormobile	B20F	1986	Ex Yorkshire Rider, 1992
D774JUB	Freight Rover Sherpa 374	Dormobile	B20F	1986	Ex Yorkshire Rider, 1992
D884MWR	Freight Rover Sherpa 374	Dormobile	B20F	1987	Ex Yorkshire Rider, 1991

EAGLE

Reg	Chassis	Body	Seating	Year	Notes
JOV718P	Bristol VRT/SL2/6LX	MCW	H43/33F	1976	Ex Simmonds, Crawley Down, 1988
613WHT	Leyland Leopard PSU3C/4R	Plaxton Supreme III	C53F	1976	
TNN753R	Leyland Leopard PSU3E/4R	Plaxton Supreme III	C53F	1977	Ex Skill, Nottingham, 1986
APM113T	AEC Reliance 6U2R	Plaxton Supreme IV Exp	C49F	1979	Ex London Country, 1985
APM114T	AEC Reliance 6U2R	Plaxton Supreme IV Exp	C49F	1979	Ex London Country, 1985
FPA584V	Leyland Leopard PSU3E/4R	Plaxton Supreme IV	C49F	1979	Ex Safeguard, Guildford, 1986
VWF328	Leyland Leopard PSU3E/4R	Plaxton Supreme IV	C38FT	1980	
FEL11V	Leyland Leopard PSU3E/4R	Plaxton Supreme IV Exp	C53F	1980	Ex Bere Regis & District, 1987
94SHU	Leyland Leopard PSU5C/4R	Plaxton Supreme IV	C57F	1980	
2411KR	DAF MB200DKTL600	Jonckheere Bermuda	C57F	1982	
6130EL	DAF MB200DKTL600	Plaxton Supreme V	C57F	1982	
24THU	Leyland Tiger TRCTL11/3R	Plaxton Supreme V	C49FT	1982	
FIL9220	DAF MB200DKFL600	Jonckheere Jubilee P50	C53F	1984	Ex Roman City, Bath, 1991
FIL9370	DAF MB200DKFL600	Jonckheere Jubilee P50	C53F	1984	Ex Roman City, Bath, 1991
863EXX	Leyland Royal Tiger B50	Van Hool Alizée	C53F	1986	
C687CNF	Freight Rover Sherpa 365	Made-to-Measure	C16F	1986	
D62NOF	Freight Rover Sherpa 365	Carlyle	B18F	1986	Ex James, Aughton, 1991
D141NON	Freight Rover Sherpa 365	Carlyle	B18F	1986	Ex Wessex, Bristol, 1991
D194NON	Freight Rover Sherpa 365	Carlyle	B18F	1986	Ex Bee Line, 1991
D935SUD	Mercedes-Benz L307D	Reeve Burgess	C12F	1987	
931DHT	DAF MB230DKLT615	Van Hool Alizée	C53F	1988	
E589LTC	DAF SB2305DHTD585	Plaxton Paramount 3200 III	C57F	1988	
E300OMG	Mercedes-Benz 609D	Reeve Burgess Beaver	DP25F	1988	
E347EVH	DAF SB3000DVK601	Van Hool Alizée	C55FT	1988	Ex Austin, Earlston, 1992
E351EVH	DAF SB3000DVK601	Van Hool Alizée	C55FT	1988	Ex Austin, Earlston, 1992
G158XJF	MAN 10-180	Caetano Algarve	C35F	1990	
H731BHW	DAF SB2305DHTD585	Plaxton Paramount 3200 III	C53F	1990	
J888ALL	Leyland Tiger TRCL10/3ARZM	Plaxton Paramount 3200 III	C57F	1991	
J811FOU	DAF 400	Carlyle Citybus 2	DP20F	1991	
J812FOU	Mercedes-Benz 814D	Carlyle	DP29F	1991	
J693GTC	DAF MB230LB615	Van Hool Alizée	C57F	1992	

Previous Registrations:

2411KR	WRK4X	863EXX	C320CWS	FIL9220	A378UNH
24THU	KHT215X	913DHT	E638KCX	FIL9370	A379UNH
6130EL	LWS116Y	94SHU	BEU809V	VWF328	DFB382W
613WHT	LHT694P				

Special Liveries:
Overall Advertisements: 613WHT, JOV718P, APM113T, TNN753R, D194NON.

FILER'S (Ilfracombe)

Reg	Chassis	Body	Seating	Year	Notes
THM548M	Daimler Fleetline CRL6	MCW	H44/32F	1973	Ex Somerbus, Paulton, 1991
NNW97P	Leyland Leopard PSU4C/4R	Duple Dominant	C45F	1976	Ex Grimmet, Carhampton, 1989
UGR378R	Bedford YLQ	Plaxton Supreme III Exp	C45F	1976	Ex Born, Chulmleigh, 1992
OUC30R	Leyland Fleetline FE30ALR	MCW	H44/24D	1976	Ex London Transport, 1985
OUC33R	Leyland Fleetline FE30AGR	MCW	H44/35F	1976	Ex Country Bus, Atherington, 1990
THX634S	Leyland Fleetline FE30ALR Sp	Park Royal	H44/27D	1977	Ex London Buses, 1991
URL856S	Leyland Leopard PSU3E/4R	Duple Dominant II	C53F	1978	Ex Westward Travel, Hayle 1990
NBF516V	Leyland Leopard PSU3E/4R	Duple Dominant II	C53F	1979	Ex Rover Coaches, Horsley, 1988
EAV814V	Volvo B58-56	Duple Dominant II	C53F	1980	Ex Bodman, Worton, 1989
HSV379	Leyland Leopard PSU5D/5R	Duple Dominant IV	C53F	1982	Ex Dunn-Line, Nottingham, 1989
RPB952X	Leyland Leopard PSU3G/4R	Eastern Coach Works B51	C49F	1982	Ex The Bee Line, 1990
RPB953X	Leyland Leopard PSU3G/4R	Eastern Coach Works B51	C49F	1982	Ex The Bee Line, 1990
682FUV	DAF MB200DKFL600	Plaxton Paramount 3200	C51FT	1983	Ex Tourmaster, Loughborough, 1987
FDZ982	Leyland Tiger TRCTL11/3R	Duple Goldliner	C51F	1982	Ex Crown Coaches, Bristol, 1992
567GOP	Volvo B10M-61	Plaxton Paramount 3500	C49FT	1984	Ex Wallace Arnold, 1990
978VYD	Volvo B10M-61	Plaxton Paramount 3500	C49FT	1984	Ex Wallace Arnold, 1990
A324XHE	Leyland Royal Tiger B54	Plaxton Paramount 3500	C49FT	1984	Ex White Hart, Bratton Fleming, 1992
B125PEL	Volvo B10M-61	Duple Dominant IV	C51F	1984	Ex Brixham Travel, 1992
B578LPE	Leyland Olympian ONTL11/2RSp	Eastern Coach Works	CH45/28F	1985	Ex Alder Valley, 1991
E562MAC	Peugeot-Talbot Pullman	Talbot	DP24F	1987	Ex Dunstan & Bruckshaw, 1990
E964SVU	Freight Rover Sherpa 365	Made-to-Measure	C18F	1987	
E442YLG	Freight Rover Sherpa 374	Carlyle Citybus 2	B20F	1987	Ex Bee Line Buzz, 1990
E686UND	Peugeot-Talbot Express	Made-to-Measure	C14F	1987	Ex Gourd, Teignmouth, 1989
F404CKU	Mercedes-Benz 609D	Whittaker	C24F	1988	

G869APJ	Mercedes-Benz 609D	Crystals	C24F	1989

Previous Registrations:

682FUV	DVS163Y	HSV379	HEC357X	URL856S	WRO447S, XRL965
FDZ982	OHM835Y	NBF516V	GRF221V, 5702PL		

FORD

HVJ146N	Bedford YRQ	Duple Dominant	B47F	1975	Ex Ffoshelig Motors, Newchurch, 1992
MPT292P	Leyland Atlantean AN68/1R	Eastern Coach Works	H45/27D	1975	Ex Oxford, 1991
MPT315P	Leyland Atlantean AN68/1R	Eastern Coach Works	H45/27D	1975	Ex Oxford, 1991
MGL64P	Bedford YMT	Plaxton Supreme III Exp	C53F	1976	Ex Jennings, Bude, 1992
WUF955	Volvo B58-61	Plaxton Supreme III	C57F	1978	Ex Goode, West Bromwich, 1990
FGL246V	Ford R1014	Duple Dominant II	C45F	1980	Ex Townsend, Bestwood, 1989
OYA695V	Volvo B58-61	Plaxton Supreme IV	C51F	1980	Ex Field, Paulton, 1991
228FHT	Volvo B10M-61	Van Hool Alizée	C50FT	1984	Ex Hand, Horsley, 1990
353TPF	Leyland Tiger TRCTL11/3RZ	Van Hool Alizée	C57F	1985	Ex Shearings, 1989
D64MWO	Leyland Tiger TRCTL11/3RZ	Plaxton Paramount 3200 III	C53F	1986	Ex Hills, Tredegar, 1992
D500NYS	Hestair Duple 425	Duple 425	C61F	1986	Ex Hutchison, Overtown, 1991
H487FGL	Volvo B10M-60	Van Hool Alizée	C37FT	1990	

Previous Registrations:

228FHT	YWD687, A239LFH	FGL246V	FRR585V, WSV537
353TPF	B311UNB	RTA637M	YJH709M, 8405CD
AEF785A	DCA767S, FXU355, FSF236S	WUF955	BGG166S

FOSSEWAY

UAD95X	Ford Transit 190	Richardson	B12F	1982	
SNL550Y	Ford Transit 190	Dormobile	B16F	1983	Ex South Wales, 1990
B202GNL	Ford Transit 190	Alexander AM	B16F	1984	Ex Go-Ahead Northern, 1991
FIB2734	Iveco Daily 49.10	Robin Hood	B21F	1985	Ex Bunston & Bruckshaw, 1991
C425AHT	Ford Transit 190	Carlyle	B16F	1985	Ex Go-Ahead Northern, 1990
C165VRE	Ford Transit 190	PMT	DP16F	1985	Ex Go-Ahead Northern, 1991
C909AHU	Ford Transit 190	Pickford	B12F	1985	
C486BFB	Ford Transit 190	Dormobile	B16F	1985	Ex Badgerline, 1991
C311RPE	Ford Transit 190	Carlyle	B16F	1985	Ex Alder Valley, 1988
C336RPE	Ford Transit 190	Carlyle	B16F	1986	Ex Alder Valley, 1988
D580VBV	Freight Rover Sherpa 374	Dormobile	B16F	1986	Ex Ribble, 1988
D169BEH	Ford Transit 190	PMT	B16F	1986	Ex PMT, 1989
D832UTF	Ford Transit 190	Carlyle	B16F	1986	Ex The Bee Line, 1989
D327WPE	Ford Transit 190	Carlyle	B16F	1986	Ex Alder Valley, 1989
D338WPE	Ford Transit 190	Carlyle	B16F	1986	Ex Alder Valley, 1989
D552HNW	Iveco Daily 49.10	Robin Hood	B21F	1986	Ex Yorkshire Rider, 1991
D559HNW	Iveco Daily 49.10	Robin Hood	B21F	1986	Ex Yorkshire Rider, 1991
D563HNW	Iveco Daily 49.10	Robin Hood	B21F	1986	Ex Yorkshire Rider, 1991
D857OJA	Freight Rover Sherpa 374	Made-to-Measure	B16F	1987	
G137GOL	Iveco Daily 49.8	Carlyle Dailybus 2	B21F	1990	Ex Taylor, Nuthampstead, 1991

Previous Registrations:

FIB2734	C516DYM

HOPLEY'S

GOU127N	Ford R1114	Duple Dominant	C53F	1975	Ex Brown & Davies, 1981
NNK808P	Bedford YRT	Duple Dominant	B66F	1975	Ex Roselyn Par, 1988
TYU499S	Bedford YMT	Plaxton Supreme III	C53F	1978	Ex Barrow, Hull, 1985
VCU899Y	Bedford YNT	Plaxton Paramount 3200	C53F	1983	Ex Jewitt, Middleton, 1991
J760KGL	Mazda E2300	Howletts	B15F	1991	

Previous Registrations:

VCU899Y	TJR784Y

KILMINGTON

KRO644V	Ford Transit 190	Dormobile	B16F	1979	Ex Mullover, Bedford, 1989
AEE513W	Bedford VAS5	Duple Dominant	C29F	1980	Ex Gourd, Kilmington, 1988
MYE425X	Ford Transit 130	Robin Hood	B12F	1982	Ex Gourd, Kilmington, 1988
TRR744X	Renault-Dodge S56	Reeve Burgess	C25F	1982	Ex LB of Hammersmith, 1988
A36HGW	Ford Transit 130	Tricentrol	B12F	1984	Ex Mullover, Bedford, 1989
A373HNF	Ford Transit 190	Dormobile	C16F	1984	Ex Gourd, Kilmington, 1988
B440WUL	Ford R1115	Wadham Stringer Vanguard	DP33F	1984	Ex Marton, West Drayton, 1988
C200WGV	Renault-Dodge S56	East Lancashire	B21F	1986	Ex Ipswich, 1990
D586EWS	Freight Rover Sherpa 374	Dormobile	DP16F	1986	Ex Badgerline, 1989
D772JUB	Freight Rover Sherpa 374	Carlyle	B20F	1986	Ex Yorkshire Rider, 1991
D911PRJ	Ford Transit 190	Made-to-Measure	DP14F	1987	Ex Gourd, Teignmouth, 1989
D471UHC	Renault-Dodge S56	East Lancashire	B24F	1987	Ex Ipswich, 1991
F309RVT	Freight Rover Sherpa 365	PMT	B20F	1988	Ex PMT, 1989
G93SVM	DAF 400	Made-to-Measure	DP16F	1990	

MAYBURY'S

KUC194P	Daimler Fleetline CRL6	Park Royal	H44/33F	1975	Ex London Sightseeing, 1987
KUC935P	Daimler Fleetline CRL6	MCW	O44/32F	1975	Ex Wilts & Dorset, 1992
KUC904P	Daimler Fleetline CRL6	MCW	H44/24D	1975	Ex London Buses, 1990
KJD21P	Leyland Fleetline FE30ALR	MCW	H44/24D	1976	Ex London Sightseeing, 1990
AUD463R	Bristol VRT/SL3/6LXB	Eastern Coach Works	H43/31F	1977	Ex Thames Transit, 1989
OKW510R	Leyland Fleetline FE30AGR	MCW	H46/25D	1977	Ex Ribble, 1990
OKW512R	Leyland Fleetline FE30AGR	MCW	H46/25D	1977	Ex Ribble, 1990
FPR668V	Bedford YMT	Duple Dominant II	C53F	1979	
NPV306W	Bedford YMT	Duple Dominant IV	C53F	1980	Ex Smith, Rayne, 1986
C717KCA	Fiat 35.10	Mellor	C14F	1986	Ex Kian, Annan, 1988
C357KEP	Auwaerter Neoplan N722/3	Plaxton Paramount 4000 II	CH53/18CT	1986	Ex South Wales, 1989
PIJ601	Auwaerter Neoplan N722/3	Plaxton Paramount 4000 II	CH53/18CT	1986	Ex South Wales, 1989
D775LUG	Freight Rover Sherpa 350	Optare	DP16F	1987	Ex Renyard, Totton, 1989
F492WPR	Dennis Javelin 12SDA1907	Duple 320	C57F	1989	
F625SAY	Dennis Javelin 12SDA1907	Duple 320	C55F	1989	
F239OFP	Dennis Javelin 12SDA1907	Duple 320	C54F	1989	Ex Dennis demonstrator, 1990
J245MFP	Dennis Javelin 12SDA1929	Plaxton Paramount 3200 III	C53F	1992	

Previous Registrations:

PIJ601	300CUH, C366KEP, LST873	C357KEP	WCY701

Named vehicles:
C717KCA *Cranborne Chaser*, D775LUG *Cranborne Chaser*.

Special Liveries:
Overall Advertisements: KUC935P

OAKFIELD TRAVEL

Note 's' indicates the Stanbridge & Crichel fleet.

s	OLE583E	AEC Reliance 2U3RA	Plaxton Panorama I	C53F	1967	Ex Ironside, Sevenoaks, 1984
s	OKE398F	AEC Reliance 6U3RA	Plaxton Panorama I	C53F	1968	Ex Ironside, Sevenoaks, 1984
s	OCK370K	Bristol RESL6L	Eastern Coach Works	B47F	1971	Ex Pennine Blue, Denton, 1991
	SWY336L	Bedford YRT	Willowbrook	B55F	1972	Ex Oakfield Travel, Blandford, 1989
s	NTY226M	AEC Reliance 6U3ZR	Duple Dominant	C57F	1973	Ex Marsh, Wincanton, 1990
	AHN604M	Bristol LH6L	Eastern Coach Works	B43F	1974	Ex Tees & District, 1992
s	GCK251N	AEC Reliance 6U3ZR	Plaxton Elite Express III	C53F	1974	Ex Lawrence, Hillingdon, 1985
	HJT37N	Bristol LH6L	Eastern Coach Works	B43F	1975	Ex Somerbus, Paulton, 1992
s	GDY550N	Bedford YRT	Duple Dominant	C53F	1974	Ex Oakfield Travel, Blandford, 1989
s	VUV246	Leyland Leopard PSU3C/4R	Duple Dominant	C53F	1975	Ex Knights Coaches, Harrow Weald, 1990
s	OYC241P	Ford R1114	Plaxton Supreme	C53F	1975	Ex Barry, Weymouth, 1991
	KDW706P	Bristol RESL6L	East Lancashire	B47F	1975	Ex Cambrian Coast, Tywyn, 1991
s	TSC916R	Bedford YRT	Duple Dominant	C45F	1976	Ex Barry, Weymouth, 1990
	RGS92R	Leyland Leopard PSU5A/4R	Plaxton Supreme III	C57F	1976	Ex Jones, Llandeilo, 1986
	TPJ66S	Bristol LHS6L	Eastern Coach Works	B35F	1977	Ex Busways, 1992
s	PVB800S	Leyland Leopard PSU3E/4R	Duple Dominant	C49F	1978	Ex Waywing, Bognor, 1991
	701GOO	AEC Reliance 6U3ZR	Van Hool	C53F	1979	Ex Vaughan, Salfords, 1987

	4078RU	MAN SR280	MAN	C53F	1979	Acquired 1992
	WTX528T	Ford A0609	Alexander AS	B28F	1978	Ex Williams, Camborne, 1989
s	KGK718T	Ford Transit 190	Ford	B12F	1979	Acquired 1990
	362KHT	MAN SR280	MAN	C53F	1979	Ex Carnell, Sheffield, 1984
	YUD652V	Bedford YMT	Van Hool	C53F	1979	Ex Carterton Coaches, 1987
	YUD655V	Bedford YMT	Van Hool	C53F	1979	Ex Carterton Coaches, 1987
	AWS488V	Volkswagen LT28	Devon Conversions	B12R	1980	Ex Lewis, Long Ashton, 1986
	PRO450W	AEC Reliance 6U3ZR	Van Hool	C50F	1980	Ex Mackie, Alloa, 1990
s	RLN775W	MAN SR280	MAN	C53F	1981	Ex Carnell, Sheffield, 1984
	XHR748A	Bedford YNT	Duple Dominant IV	C53F	1982	Ex Beeline, Warminster, 1990

Previous Registrations:

362KHT	NLC870V	701GOO	FKX289T	XHR748A	YUD655V
4078RU	JLS5V	VUV246	MDF119P		

PROUT

RBD116M	Bedford YRT	Willowbrook	B53F	1974	Ex Striplin, Tavistock, 1985
URD890N	Bedford YRQ	Willowbrook	B45F	1974	Ex Roselyn, Par, 1988
HAF430N	Bedford YRT	Duple Dominant	C53F	1975	Ex Rowe, Dobwalls, 1979
SUR284R	Leyland Leopard PSU3C/4R	Plaxton Supreme III	C49F	1977	Ex Webber, Blisland, 1992
SAD122R	Leyland Leopard PSU3C/4R	Duple Dominant	C53F	1977	Ex Burrows, Ogmore Vale, 1988
AFH390T	Bedford YMT	Duple Dominant II	C53F	1978	Ex Warner, Tewkesbury, 1984
385UFM	Volvo B58-61	Duple Dominant II	C57F	1980	Ex Coliseum, West End, 1988
LVO45W	Leyland Leopard PSU5D/5R	Duple Dominant II	C50F	1980	Ex Waters, Addlestone, 1986

Previous Registrations: 385UFM YPX113V

PULHAM'S

HDF700L	Leyland Leopard PSU3B/4R	Plaxton Elite III	C53F	1973	
DDD200T	Leyland Leopard PSU3E/4R	Plaxton Supreme IV Exp	C53F	1979	
HAD888V	Leyland Leopard PSU3E/4R	Plaxton Supreme IV Exp	C53F	1979	
NAD600W	Leyland Leopard PSU3E/4R	Plaxton Supreme IV Exp	C53F	1980	
NFH200W	Leyland Leopard PSU3E/4R	Plaxton Supreme IV Exp	C49F	1980	
VDG700X	Leyland Leopard PSU3F/4R	Plaxton Supreme IV EXp	C49F	1982	
CFX427Y	Ford Transit 190	Yeates	B12F	1983	Ex Fawcett, Mere, 1986
DAD600Y	Leyland Tiger TRCTL11/3R	Plaxton Paramount 3200	C57F	1983	
DDD122Y	Leyland Tiger TRCTL11/3R	Plaxton Paramount 3200	C57F	1983	
RMO201Y	Leyland Tiger TRCTL11/2R	Plaxton Paramount 3200 E	C53F	1983	Ex Reading, 1991
RMO202Y	Leyland Tiger TRCTL11/2R	Plaxton Paramount 3200 E	C53F	1983	Ex Reading, 1991
RMO204Y	Leyland Tiger TRCTL11/2R	Plaxton Paramount 3200 E	C53F	1983	Ex Reading, 1991
A748JAY	Leyland Tiger TRCTL11/2R	Plaxton Paramount 3200 E	C49F	1984	Ex Pilcher, Strood, 1986
B333SDD	Mercedes-Benz L608D	PMT	C21F	1985	
C71XDG	Leyland Tiger TRCTL11/3R	Plaxton P'mount 3200(1989)	C53F	1986	
C193CYO	Volvo B10M-46	Plaxton Paramount 3200 II	C37F	1986	Ex Tellings, Byfleet, 1989
F150RFH	Volvo B10M-61	Plaxton Paramount 3500 III	C49FT	1988	
F401UAD	Volvo B10M-61	Plaxton Paramount 3500 III	C49FT	1989	
H345KDF	Volvo B10M-60	Plaxton Paramount 3200 III	C55F	1991	
J914MDG	Volvo B10M-60	Plaxton Paramount 3200 III	C57F	1991	

RED BUS SERVICES

1	XTA839	Albion Nimbus NS3N	Willowbrook	B31F	1958	Ex Hazell, Wellington, 1982
2	WWY125S	Bristol VRT/SL3/6LXB	Eastern Coach Works	H43/31F	1978	Ex York City & Dist, 1990
3	ECS844S	Seddon Pennine 7	Alexander AY	B51F	1978	Ex Lowland Scottish, 1988
4	J844NOD	Mercedes-Benz 811D	Wadham Stringer	B33F	1991	
6	RCS703R	Seddon Pennine 7	Alexander AT	B49F	1978	Ex North East, Gateshead, 1989
7	ECS847S	Seddon Pennine 7	Alexander AY	B51F	1978	Ex Lowland Scottish, 1988
8	YWY828S	Bristol VRT/SL3/6LXB	Eastern Coach Works	H43/31F	1978	Ex Keighley & Dist, 1990
9	NNW120P	Leyland Leopard PSU3C/4R	Duple Dominant	C53F	1976	Acquired 1991
550	VOD550K	Bristol VRT/SL6G	Eastern Coach Works	H43/31F	1972	Ex Western National, 1991

Special Liveries: Devon General: 550

ROSELYN

241AJB	AEC Regent V 2D3RA	Park Royal	H41/31F	1962	Ex AERE, Harwell, 1983
BJV104L	Daimler Fleetline CRG6LX	Roe	H45/29D	1973	Ex Derby, 1989
OCH260L	Daimler Fleetline CRG6LX	Roe	H44/34F	1973	Ex Derby, 1988
OCH261L	Daimler Fleetline CRG6LX	Roe	H44/34F	1973	Ex Derby, 1989
OCH271L	Daimler Fleetline CRG6LX	Roe	H44/34F	1973	Ex Derby, 1989
URD889N	Bedford YRQ	Willowbrook	B45F	1974	Ex AERE, Harwell, 1988
NNK809P	Bedford YRT	Duple Dominant	B66F	1976	Ex AERE, Harwell, 1988
244AJB	AEC Reliance 6U3ZR	Plaxton Supreme III	C57F	1976	Ex Green, South Molton, 1980
TMW997S	AEC Reliance 6U2R	Duple Dominant II Exp	C53F	1978	Ex M C Travel, Melksham, 1991
239AJB	Volvo B58-56	Plaxton Supreme IV Exp	C53F	1981	
B345VTA	Renault-Dodge S56	Reeve Burgess	B21F	1985	Ex Plymouth Citybus, 1991
E44SAF	Volvo B10M-61	Van Hool Alizée	C53F	1988	
H825ERV	Mercedes-Benz 709D	Wadham Stringer	B27F	1990	Ex WS demonstrator, 1991
J6EDE	Mercedes-Benz 709D	Wadham Stringer	B21F	1991	

Previous Registrations:

239AJB	KAF129W	244AJB	MUN942R	TMW997S	VPH57S, 701CGA

RYAN

NUD106L	Bristol VRT/SL6G	Eastern Coach Works	O41/27F	1972	Ex South Midland, 1989
THM538M	Daimler Fleetline CRL6	MCW	O44/24D	1974	Ex South Midland, 1989
GHV121N	Daimler Fleetline CRL6	Park Royal	O45/27D	1975	Ex South Midland, 1989
TNJ996S	Bristol VRT/SL3/6LXB	Eastern Coach Works	O43/27D	1977	Ex Brighton & Hove, 1990
ELR108T	Bedford YMT	Plaxton Supreme IV	C53F	1977	Ex Kirby, High Wycombe, 1988
NRR36W	Bedford YMT	Plaxton Supreme IV	C53F	1979	Ex Simons Coaches, 1992
LFG248W	Bristol LHS6L	Plaxton Supreme IV	C35F	1980	Ex Green, Kirkintilloch, 1989
HHR1W	Bedford YMT	Duple Dominant IV	C53F	1981	Ex Thomas, Calne, 1992
PNW313W	Leyland Leopard PSU3F/4R	Plaxton Supreme IV	C49F	1980	Ex Athelstan, Chippenham, 1990
NXI608	Leyland Tiger TRCTL11/3R	Plaxton Supreme IV	C53F	1981	Ex Jorvik, York, 1992
HHY575X	Mercedes-Benz L207D	Devon Conversions	C12F	1982	Ex Bennett, Bath, 1988
ANA565Y	Leyland Atlantean AN68D/1R	Northern Counties	O43/32F	1983	Ex GM Buses, 1991
A330XHE	Leyland Royal Tiger B50	Plaxton Paramount 3500	C47FT	1984	Ex Crown, Bristol, 1991
D353SNS	Freight Rover Sherpa 365	Scott	C16F	1986	Ex Stirling, Kilsyth, 1989
D595MVR	Leyland Tiger TRCTL11/3RZ	Plaxton Paramount 3200 III	C53F	1987	Ex Shearings, 1992

Previous Registrations:
544UYD   From new

Named Vehicles:
ANA565Y *Hannah.*

SAFEWAY

ASV900	Dennis Lancet III	Reading	C33F	1949	
GIB5970	Leyland Leopard PSU3E/4R	Willowbrook Warrior (1992)	B55F	1985	Acquired 1992
PYC746L	Leyland Leopard PSU3B/4R	Willowbrook	B53F	1973	
RYA676L	Leyland Leopard PSU3B/4R	Willowbrook	B53F	1973	
UAR940M	Leyland Leopard PSU3B/4R	Plaxton Elite III	C53F	1974	Ex Grant, Fareham, 1978
VPF42M	Leyland Leopard PSU3B/4R	Willowbrook	B53F	1974	Ex Safeguard, Guildford, 1982
OGR654P	Leyland Leopard PSU3C/4R	Willowbrook	B55F	1976	Ex Ford, Ackworth, 1984
TYD911W	Leyland Leopard PSU3F/5R	Duple Dominant IV	B61F	1980	
VYC852W	Leyland Leopard PSU3F/4R	Duple Dominant II	C53F	1981	
NPA228W	Leyland Leopard PSU3F/4R	Plaxton Supreme IV Exp	C49F	1981	Ex London Country, 1986
YYA122X	Leyland Leopard PSU3F/4R	Plaxton Supreme IV	C53F	1982	
FHA609Y	Leyland Tiger TRCTL11/2R	Duple Dominant IV	C49F	1983	Ex Ludlow, Halesowen, 1992
A983NYC	Leyland Tiger TRCTL11/2R	Plaxton Paramount 3200	C53F	1983	
C744JYA	Leyland Tiger TRCTL11/3RZ	Willowbrook Crusader	C55F	1986	
E565YYA	Leyland Tiger TRCTL11/3RZ	Duple 320	C55F	1988	

Previous Registrations:
GIB5970   XCW153R

SOMERBUS

18	C618JHS	Toyota HB31R	Caetano Optimo	C21F	1986	Acquired 1992
24	LUA324V	Leyland National 2 NL106L11/1R		B41F	1980	Ex Stevenson, Uttoxeter, 1992
25	C825CBU	Renault-Dodge S56	Northern Counties	B18F	1986	Ex GM Buses, 1991
28	LUA328V	Leyland National 2 NL106L11/1R		B41F	1980	Ex Stevenson, Uttoxeter, 1992
29	GRF702V	Bristol VRT/SL3/501	Eastern Coach Works	H43/31F	1980	Ex Blue Triangle, Bootle, 1992
35	MNM35V	Leyland Leopard PSU3E/4R	Plaxton Supreme	C53F	1980	Ex Oates, St Ives, 1992
52	DCM552X	Leyland Tiger TRCTL11/3R	Duple Dominant	C53F	1982	Ex Price, Newcastle, 1992
	J499GHU	Ford Transit VE6	Ford	C11C	1992	

Named vehicles:
24 *Rosie*, 35 *Tudor Rose*

STREAMLINE

B570ABH	Ford Transit 190	Trimoco	B12F	1984	Ex Dewberry, Biggin Hill, 1988
C319OFL	Ford Transit 190	Dormobile	B16F	1985	Ex Viscount, Cambridge, 1990
C323OFL	Ford Transit 190	Dormobile	B16F	1985	Ex Viscount, Cambridge, 1990
C124ADD	Volvo B10M-46	Plaxton Paramount 3200 II	C36F	1986	Ex Davis, Minchinhampton, 1992
D514NDA	Freight Rover Sherpa 365	Carlyle	B18F	1986	Ex Dunstan, Davenport, 1991
D194LRJ	Freight Rover Sherpa 350	Made-to-Measure	B16F	1986	
D195LRJ	Freight Rover Sherpa 350	Made-to-Measure	B16F	1986	
D556MVR	Volvo B10M-61	Van Hool Alizée	C53F	1987	Ex Shearings, 1992
D201KWT	Freight Rover Sherpa 374	Dormobile	B16F	1987	Ex West Riding, 1988
D203KWT	Freight Rover Sherpa 374	Dormobile	B16F	1987	Ex West Riding, 1988
F965DKP	Iveco Daily 49.10	Dormobile Routemaker	B21F	1988	
F991DKO	Iveco Daily 49.10	Dormobile Routemaker	B25F	1988	
G229EOA	Iveco Daily 49.10	Carlyle Dailybus 2	B25F	1989	
K695RNR	Toyota Coaster HDB30R	Caetano Optimo II	C21F	1992	

SWANBROOK

NOB306M	Daimler Fleetline CRG6LX	Park Royal	H43/33F	1973	Ex West Midlands, 1986
KDF100P	Bedford YRT	Duple Dominant	DP57F	1975	
NNN10P	AEC Reliance 6U2R	Plaxton Supreme III Exp	C53F	1976	Ex Derby, 1987
TDF103R	Bedford YMT	Plaxton Supreme III Exp	C53F	1977	
MVK546R	Leyland Atlantean AN68A/2R	Alexander AL	H48/34F	1977	Ex Colchester, 1990
MVK548R	Leyland Atlantean AN68A/2R	Alexander AL	H48/34F	1977	Ex Colchester, 1990
OJD151R	Leyland Fleetline FE30AGR	Park Royal	H44/29F	1976	Ex Stevenson, Spath, 1992
SDA566S	Leyland Fleetline FE30AGR	Park Royal	H43/33F	1977	Ex West Midlands Travel, 1992
SDA644S	Leyland Fleetline FE30AGR	Park Royal	H43/33F	1977	Ex West Midlands Travel, 1990
SDA659S	Leyland Fleetline FE30AGR	Park Royal	H43/33F	1977	Ex West Midlands Travel, 1990
SDA776S	Leyland Fleetline FE30AGR	Park Royal	H43/33F	1978	Ex West Midlands Travel, 1992
WFH105S	Bedford YMT	Plaxton Supreme III Exp	C53F	1978	
ADF106T	Bedford YMT	Plaxton Supreme IV Exp	C53F	1978	
ADF107T	Bedford YMT	Plaxton Supreme IV Exp	C53F	1978	
FDD109T	Bedford YMT	Plaxton Supreme IV Exp	C53F	1979	
FDD110T	Bedford YMT	Plaxton Supreme IV Exp	C53F	1979	
XHR405T	Bedford YMT	Duple Dominant II	C53F	1979	Ex Rimes, Swindon, 1985
XHR406T	Bedford YMT	Duple Dominant II	C53F	1979	Ex Rimes, Swindon, 1985
XHR407T	Bedford YMT	Duple Dominant II	C53F	1979	Ex O'Byrne, Cheltenham, 1989
JDG111V	Bedford YMT	Plaxton Supreme IV Exp	C53F	1980	
JDG112V	Bedford YMT	Plaxton Supreme IV Exp	C53F	1980	
MIB5088	Leyland Leopard PSU3F/4R	Willowbrook Warrior (1989)	B53F	1981	Ex United Counties, 1990
C179LWB	Volvo B10M-61	Plaxton Paramount 3500 II	C53F	1987	Ex Clarke, London SE20, 1992
C954KSD	Volvo B10M-61	Plaxton Paramount 3500 II	C52F	1987	Ex Stonehouse, Larkhall, 1991
D120EFH	Hestair Duple 425	Duple 425	C59FT	1987	
D122EFH	Bedford YMT	Plaxton Derwent	B55F	1987	
D123EFH	Bedford YMT	Plaxton Derwent	B55F	1987	
E206EPB	Hestair Duple 425	Duple 425	C57F	1987	Ex Alder Valley, 1992
E207EPB	Hestair Duple 425	Duple 425	C57F	1987	Ex Alder Valley, 1992
E208EPB	Hestair Duple 425	Duple 425	C57F	1987	Ex Alder Valley, 1992
E126LAD	Hestair Duple 425	Duple 425	C51FT	1988	
E127LAD	Hestair Duple 425	Duple 425	C51FT	1988	
F129TDF	Hestair Duple 425	Duple 425	C51FT	1988	
F130TDF	Hestair Duple 425	Duple 425	C51FT	1988	

G837GNV	Volvo B10M-60	Jonckheere Deauville	C51FT	1990	Ex Tellings-Golden Miller, 1992
H131JFH	Van Hool T815H	Van Hool Alizée	C49FT	1991	
H132JFH	Volvo B10M-60	Ikarus Blue Danube	C49FT	1991	

Operators:
F129TDF is operated by Mrs Wiggin, an associate of Swanbrook and is in Swanbrook livery.

Previous Registrations:

C954KSD	OFA950	MIB5088	CNH172X

Special Liveries:
Overall Advertisements: NOB306M, MVK546/8R, SDA566/776S

TALLY HO!

POD829H	Bristol RELL6G	Eastern Coach Works	B53F	1969	Ex Devon General, 1984
POD830H	Bristol RELL6G	Eastern Coach Works	B53F	1969	Ex Devon General, 1984
TWX193L	Bristol RELL6G	Eastern Coach Works	B53F	1973	Ex Norfolk, Nayland, 1990
NWU324M	Bristol RELL6G	Eastern Coach Works	B53F	1974	Ex Norfolk, Nayland, 1990
WUO505	Ford R1014	Duple Dominant	C45F	1975	
KJD410P	Bristol LH6L	Eastern Coach Works	B39F	1976	Ex London Buses, 1986
KJD413P	Bristol LH6L	Eastern Coach Works	B39F	1976	Ex London Transport, 1982
KJD414P	Bristol LH6L	Eastern Coach Works	B39F	1976	Ex London Buses, 1986
KJD419P	Bristol LH6L	Eastern Coach Works	B39F	1976	Ex London Buses, 1992
KJD420P	Bristol LH6L	Eastern Coach Works	B39F	1976	Ex London Transport, 1982
KJD422P	Bristol LH6L	Eastern Coach Works	B39F	1976	Ex London Buses, 1986
KJD423P	Bristol LH6L	Eastern Coach Works	B39F	1976	Ex London Transport, 1982
NOD952P	Ford R1114	Duple Dominant	C53F	1976	
OJD45R	Bristol LH6L	Eastern Coach Works	B39F	1976	Ex Tyne & Wear, Gateshead, 1990
OJD51R	Bristol LH6L	Eastern Coach Works	B39F	1976	Ex London Transport, 1982
OJD56R	Bristol LH6L	Eastern Coach Works	B39F	1976	Ex Tyne & Wear, Gateshead, 1990
OJD58R	Bristol LH6L	Eastern Coach Works	B39F	1976	Ex London Transport, 1982
OJD59R	Bristol LH6L	Eastern Coach Works	B39F	1977	Ex London Transport, 1982
OJD77R	Bristol LH6L	Eastern Coach Works	B39F	1977	Ex London Transport, 1982
OSR192R	Bristol VRT/LL3/6LXB	Alexander AL	H49/34D	1977	Ex Tayside, 1981
OSR194R	Bristol VRT/LL3/6LXB	Alexander AL	H49/34D	1977	Ex Tayside, 1981
OSR204R	Bristol VRT/LL3/6LXB	Alexander AL	H49/34D	1977	Ex Procter, Hanley, 1983
SFJ104R	Bristol VRT/SL3/6LXB	Eastern Coach Works	H43/31F	1977	Ex Devon General, 1989
XDV604S	Bristol VRT/SL3/6LXB	Eastern Coach Works	H43/31F	1977	Ex Devon General, 1989
AFJ771T	Bristol VRT/SL3/6LXB	Eastern Coach Works	H43/31F	1978	Ex Devon General, 1989
PJS646T	Ford R1014	Duple Dominant	C45F	1978	Ex Baker, Yeovil, 1990
DKL955Y	Renault-Dodge S56	Dormobile	B20F	1979	Acquired 1991
EKR295Y	Renault-Dodge S56	Rootes	B23F	1979	Ex Kenn Garage, Clevedon, 1987
WDR598	Volvo B58-56	Unicar	C55F	1978	Ex Brennan, Bideford, 1984
312KTT	Volvo B10M-61	Berkhof Esprite 370	C49FT	1987	Ex Limebourne, London SW1, 1987
YXL947	Volvo B10M-61	Berkhof Esprite 370	C49FT	1987	Ex Limebourne, London SW1, 1987
A581OTA	Renault-Dodge S46	Dormobile	B20F	1984	Ex Kemp, Kingsbridge, 1992
C112JCS	Leyland Tiger TRCTXC/2RH	Duple 320	C49FT	1986	Ex Clydeside, 1992
C113JCS	Leyland Tiger TRCTXC/2RH	Duple 320	C49FT	1986	Ex Clydeside, 1992
E275DDV	Dennis Javelin 12SDA1907	Duple 320	C53FT	1988	
E276DDV	Dennis Javelin 12SDA1907	Duple 320	C53FT	1988	
E39SBO	Dennis Javelin 11SDA1906	Duple 320	C53F	1988	Ex Bebb, Llantwit Fardre, 1989
E40SBO	Dennis Javelin 11SDA1906	Duple 320	C53F	1988	Ex Bebb, Llantwit Fardre, 1989
F389HTA	Renault-Dodge S56	Wadham Stringer	B22FL	1988	

Previous Registrations:

312KTT	A826NTW	WUO505	JOD857N
WDR598	ACP54V	YXL947	A827NTW

TRURONIAN

RFA406J	Daimler Fleetline CRG6LX	Northern Counties	H42/33F	1970	Ex Flora Motors, Helston, 1987
NDR505J	Leyland Atlantean PDR2/1	Park Royal	H47/30D	1971	Ex Plymouth, 1987
RNA220J	Daimler Fleetline CRG6LXB	Park Royal	H47/29D	1971	Ex Flora Motors, Helston, 1987
DAR524K	Leyland Leopard PSU3B/4R	Plaxton Elite II	C51F	1972	Ex Flora Motors, Helston, 1987
FHE806L	Bristol VRT/SL2/6LX	Eastern Coach Works	H43/34F	1973	Ex RoadCar, 1991
YRC125M	Bristol VRT/SL2/6LX	Eastern Coach Works	H43/34F	1974	Ex Trent, 1992

Registration	Chassis	Body	Seating	Year	History
SPK116M	Bristol LHS6L	Eastern Coach Works	B35F	1974	Ex South Wales, 1992
SMU941N	Daimler Fleetline CRL6	Park Royal	H44/30F	1974	Ex Cherry Tree, Ruan Minor, 1991
GPD318N	Bristol LHS6L	Eastern Coach Works	B35F	1974	Ex Glenlivet & District, 1990
GHM855N	Daimler Fleetline CRL6	MCW	H44/24D	1975	Ex Brown, Truro, 1987
NCV210R	Bedford YMT	Duple Dominant	C53F	1976	Ex Brown, Truro, 1987
OJD15R	Bristol LHS6L	Eastern Coach Works	B35F	1976	Ex Glenlivet & District, 1990
PUF585R	Bristol VRT/SL3/6LXB	Eastern Coach Works	H43/31F	1976	Ex Brighton & Hove, 1991
PUF588R	Bristol VRT/SL3/6LXB	Eastern Coach Works	H43/31F	1976	Ex Brighton & Hove, 1991
SVL832R	Bristol LH6L	Eastern Coach Works	B43F	1977	Ex RoadCar, 1991
SFS159V	Leyland Atlantean AN68/2R	Alexander AL	H47/32F	1980	Ex Brown, Truro, 1987
PRC849X	Bristol VRT/SL3/6LXB	Eastern Coach Works	H43/31F	1981	Ex Trent, 1991
PRC856X	Bristol VRT/SL3/6LXB	Eastern Coach Works	H43/31F	1981	Ex Trent, 1991
B465YUR	Bedford YNV	Jonckheere Jubilee P50	C53F	1985	Ex Brown, Truro, 1987
C916DFJ	Volkswagen LT31	Devon Conversions	DP12C	1985	Ex Plymouth Citybus, 1988
C917DFJ	Volkswagen LT31	Devon Conversions	DP12C	1985	Ex Plymouth Citybus, 1988
C918DFJ	Volkswagen LT31	Devon Conversions	DP12C	1985	Ex Plymouth Citybus, 1988
C181RVV	Volvo B10M-61	Caetano Algarve	C53F	1985	Ex Harris, Armadale, 1988
E872PGL	Mercedes-Benz 609D	Reeve Burgess	DP19F	1987	
F185UGL	Volvo B10M-61	Plaxton Paramount 3500 III	C49FT	1988	
F314VCV	Mercedes-Benz 609D	Reeve Burgess Beaver	B20F	1988	
F315VCV	Mercedes-Benz 609D	Reeve Burgess Beaver	DP25F	1988	
G744BCV	DAF SB2305DHS585	Caetano Algarve	C53F	1989	
G745BCV	DAF SB2305DHS585	Caetano Algarve	C53F	1989	
J756JCV	Volvo B10M-60	Caetano Algarve	C51FT	1992	

Special Liveries:
Overall Advertisements: SMU941N, PRC856X.

WAKE'S

Registration	Chassis	Body	Seating	Year	History
SYA780L	Bedford YRT	Duple Dominant	C53F	1973	
PDV244M	Bedford YRQ	Duple Dominant	C41F	1974	Ex Tally Ho!, Kingsbridge, 1984
YYA877N	Bedford YRQ	Duple Dominant	C45F	1974	
OFA2P	Leyland Leopard PSU3/3RT	Plaxton Supreme (1976)	C51F	1976	Ex Regent, Whitstable, 1985
RYB370R	Bedford YRQ	Duple Dominant	C45F	1976	
UFL781S	Leyland Leopard PSU5C/4R	Duple Dominant	C57F	1978	Ex Morris, Pencoed, 1984
ETL545T	Bedford YRQ	Plaxton Supreme IV Exp	C45F	1978	Ex Booth, Hyde, 1987
KUP14T	Bedford YRQ	Duple Dominant	B47F	1978	Ex Osmond, Curry Rivel, 1987
LYA315V	Bedford YMT	Duple Dominant II	DP53F	1979	
WSV323	Leyland Leopard PSU5C/4R	Plaxton P'mount 3200 (1992)	C57F	1979	
NYC398V	Bedford YMT	Duple Dominant II	C53F	1980	
SYD1W	Bedford YMT	Duple Dominant II	C53F	1980	
SYD2W	Bedford YMT	Duple Dominant II	C53F	1980	
UYD950W	Bedford YRQ	Duple Dominant	B55F	1981	Ex Osmond, Curry Rivel, 1987
WYD103W	Leyland Leopard PSU3F/5R	Duple Dominant II	C53F	1981	
WYD104W	Leyland Leopard PSU3E/4R	Duple Dominant II	C53F	1981	
XBJ860	Bedford YMQ/S	Plaxton Supreme IV	C22F	1981	Ex Armchair, Brentford, 1987
OPS550X	Bedford YMQ	Duple Dominant IV	C35F	1982	Ex Mills, Baltasound, 1986
PWJ497X	Bedford YMT	Duple Dominant IV	B55F	1982	Ex Priory, Gosport, 1988
BYD795X	Leyland Leopard PSU3F/5R	Duple Dominant IV	C53F	1982	
KYA284Y	Leyland Tiger TRCTL11/3R	Plaxton Paramount 3200	C57F	1983	
FNM862Y	Leyland Tiger TRCTL11/2R	Plaxton Paramount 3200	C53F	1983	Ex Lodge, High Easter, 1989
CIB7866	Leyland Tiger TRCTL11/3R	Plaxton Paramount 3500	C49FT	1984	Ex Sargeant, Kingston, 1992
A831PPP	Leyland Tiger TRCTL11/3R	Plaxton Paramount 3200	C53F	1984	Ex Armchair, Brentford, 1987
B155AYD	Leyland Tiger TRCTL11/3R	Plaxton Paramount 3200 II	C55F	1985	
E529VYD	Mercedes-Benz 609D	Reeve Burgess Beaver	DP19F	1988	
F990FYB	Dennis Javelin 8.5SDL1903	Plaxton Paramount 3200 III	C35F	1989	
F555FYD	Volvo B10M-61	Plaxton Paramount 3200 III	C53F	1989	
G518EFX	Volvo B10M-60	Plaxton Paramount 3200 III	C53F	1990	Ex Excelsior, Bournemouth, 1992
G183OYC	Volvo B10M-60	Plaxton Paramount 3500	C53F	1990	

Previous Registrations:

CIB7866	ANA109Y	OFA2P	ECH7C	XBJ860	UUR341W
G518EFX	G520EFX	WSV323	LVS421V		

WILLIAMS

MPT317P	Leyland Atlantean AN68/1R	Eastern Coach Works	H45/27D	1973	Ex Oxford, 1991
KSU863P	Leyland Atlantean AN68A/1R	Alexander AL	H45/31F	1973	Ex Filer, Illfracombe, 1986
DCV317V	Bedford YMT	Duple Dominant II	C53F	1980	
NCV942X	Bedford YNT	Plaxton Supreme IV Exp	C53F	1982	

GUERNSEYBUS

Note – Some vehicles have been re-registered since receiving their first Guernsey plates.

MB2	49377	Ford Transit 190	Ford	B12F	1987	
MB3	44525	Ford Transit 190	Ford	B12F	1988	
MB4	14223	Mercedes-Benz L307D	Mercedes-Benz	B12F	1983	
MB5	48701	Mercedes-Benz L310	Mercedes-Benz	B12F	1983	
MB6	48706	Mercedes-Benz L310	Mercedes-Benz	B12F	1984	
MB7	18264	Freight Rover Sherpa 365	Dormobile	B16F	1986	Ex Midland Red North, 1990
MB8	18265	Freight Rover Sherpa 365	Dormobile	B16F	1986	Ex Midland Red North, 1990
MB9	18266	Freight Rover Sherpa 365	Dormobile	B16F	1986	Ex Midland Red North, 1990
MB10	18267	Freight Rover Sherpa 365	Dormobile	B16F	1986	Ex Midland Red North, 1990
MB11	29694	Freight Rover Sherpa 365	Carlyle	B18F	1986	Ex Bee Line Buzz, 1992
14	2388	AEC Regent III RT	Weymann	O30/26R	1950	Originally London Transport
15	2634	AEC Regent III RT	Park Royal	O30/26R	1950	Originally London Transport
16	2493	Leyland Tiger PS1	Guernseybus/Pariaulx (1990) OB34F		1951	Originally JMT
17	9439	Leyland Tiger PS1	Reading/Pariaulx (1992)	B34F	1951	Originally JMT
18	2972	AEC Regent III RT	Park Royal	O30/26R	1951	Originally London Transport

50-72

		Bristol LH6L	Eastern Coach Works	B43F	1975-77	Originally London Buses

50	10026	55	29732	61	9439	65	31924	69	31928
51	29728	56	29733	62	31921	66	31925	70	31929
52	29729	57	28402	63	31922	67	31926	71	31930
53	29730	59	14859	64	31923	68	31927	72	5579
54	29731	60	14857						

73	14626	Bristol LHS6L	Eastern Coach Works	B35F	1977	Originally London Country
74	19662	Bristol LHS6L	Eastern Coach Works	B35F	1974	Originally Southern Vectis
75	14531	Bristol LHS6L	Eastern Coach Works	B35F	1979	Ex Western National, 1986
76	14838	Bristol LHS6L	Eastern Coach Works	B35F	1979	Ex Western National, 1986
78	12723	Bristol LHS6L	Eastern Coach Works	B27F	1974	Ex Tayside, 1987
79	12727	Bristol LHS6L	Eastern Coach Works	B27F	1974	Ex Tayside, 1987
80	31906	Bristol LHS6L	Eastern Coach Works	B27F	1974	Ex Tayside, 1987
81	24775	Bristol LHS6L	Eastern Coach Works	B27F	1975	Ex Tayside, 1987
82	31920	Bristol LHS6L	Eastern Coach Works	DP29F	1975	Ex Tayside, 1987
83	19660	Bristol LHS6L	Eastern Coach Works	DP29F	1980	Ex National Welsh, 1987
84	19663	Bristol LHS6L	Eastern Coach Works	DP29F	1980	Ex National Welsh, 1987
85	19675	Bristol LHS6L	Eastern Coach Works	DP29F	1981	Ex National Welsh, 1987
86	19676	Bristol LHS6L	Eastern Coach Works	DP29F	1981	Ex National Welsh, 1987
87	19677	Bristol LHS6L	Eastern Coach Works	B26F	1976	Ex Day, Gorey, 1978
88	19678	Bristol LHS6L	Eastern Coach Works	B35F	1974	Originally London Country
114	25701	Bedford J6L	Pennine Coachcraft	B35F	1974	Ex Guernsey Railway, 1981
117	3338	Bedford J6L	Pennine Coachcraft	B35F	1974	Ex Guernsey Railway, 1981
157	31907	Bristol LHS6L	Plaxton Supreme III	C31F	1975	Originally Greenslades

158-171

		Bristol LH6L	Plaxton Elite III	C43F	1975	Originally Greenslades

158	31908	161	31911	164	31914	167	31917	170	Due 1992
159	31909	162	31912	165	31915	168	31918	171	Due 1992
160	31910	163	31913	166	31916	169	31919		

Previous Registrations:

2388	KXW123	19675	KWO568X	31912	JFJ505N
2493	J.5567	19676	KWO569X	31913	JFJ506N
2634	KXW476	19677	OJD12R	31914	JFJ507N
2972	LUC196	19678	GPD304N	31915	JFJ508N
5579	OJD67R	24775	MUA42P	31916	JFJ499N
9439	J.5660	28401	OJD46R	31917	JFJ500N
12723	JUG356N	28402	KJD438P	31918	JFJ501N
12727	JUG357N	29694	D126NON	31919	JFJ502N
14223	A167DOT	29728	OJD48R	31920	MUA43P
14531	FDV790V	29729	OJD64R	31921	OJD52R

14626	TPJ63S	29730	OJD94R	31922	KJD403P
14838	FDV791V	29731	KJD407P	31923	OJD50R
14857	OJD47R	29732	OJD73R	31924	OJD90R
14859	OJD72R	29733	KJD418P	31925	KJD425P
18264	D64YRF	31906	JUG355N	31926	OJD74R
18265	D66YRF	31907	JFH473N	31927	KJD437P
18266	D67YRF	31908	JFJ497N	31928	KJD417P
18267	D72YRF	31909	JFJ498N	31929	KJD430P
19660	GTX758W	31910	JFJ503N	31930	KJD432P
19663	GTX759W	31911	JFJ504N		

JERSEY

1	J15374	Leyland Swift LBM6T/2R	Wadham Stringer Vanguard	B43F	1991
2	J58917	Ford R1014	Duple Dominant	B45F	1978
3	J70700	MCW MetroRider MF158	MCW	B33F	1988
5	J15908	Leyland Swift LBM6T/2R	Wadham Stringer Vanguard	B43F	1991
6	J33700	Ford R1014	Willowbrook	B44F	1975
7	J33622	Ford R1014	Willowbrook	B44F	1975
8	J33670	Ford R1014	Willowbrook	B44F	1975
9	J33627	Ford R1014	Willowbrook	B44F	1975
11	J32066	Ford R1014	Duple Dominant	B44F	1975
12	J31120	Ford R1014	Duple Dominant	B44F	1975
14	J33617	Ford R1014	Willowbrook	B44F	1975
15	J58924	Ford R1014	Duple Dominant	B45F	1978
16	J33704	Ford R1014	Duple Dominant	B44F	1975
17	J40820	Ford R1015	Wadham Stringer Vanguard	B45F	1986
18	J40853	Ford R1015	Wadham Stringer Vanguard	B45F	1986
19	J15884	Leyland Swift LBM6T/2R	Wadham Stringer Vanguard	B43F	1991
20	J43037	Ford R1115	Wadham Stringer Vanguard	B45F	1984
21	J42653	Ford R1015	Wadham Stringer Vanguard	B45F	1985
22	J33763	Ford R1014	Duple Dominant	B44F	1975
23	J43063	Ford R1115	Wadham Stringer Vanguard	B45F	1984
24	J34191	Ford R1115	Wadham Stringer Vanguard	B45F	1984 Ex Wadham Stringer, 1985
25	J40865	Ford R1015	Wadham Stringer Vanguard	B45F	1986
26	J43066	Ford R1115	Wadham Stringer Vanguard	B45F	1984
27	J32062	Ford R1014	Duple Dominant	B45F	1975
28	J70708	MCW MetroRider MF158	MCW	B33F	1988
29	J43048	Ford R1115	Wadham Stringer Vanguard	B45F	1984

30-38

		Ford R1014	Duple Dominant	B45F	1980-82

30	J14639	32	J14645	34	J29709	36	J29713	38	J58921
31	J14644	33	J14650	35	J29710	37	J29717		

39	J40899	Ford R1015	Wadham Stringer Vanguard	B45F	1986
40	J15079	Ford R1014	Duple Dominant	B41F	1977
41	J42252	Ford R1115	Wadham Stringer Vanguard	B45F	1985
42	J42259	Ford R1115	Wadham Stringer Vanguard	B45F	1985
43	J42998	Ford R1115	Wadham Stringer Vanguard	B45F	1985
44	J15031	Ford R1014	Duple Dominant	B41F	1977
45	J70712	MCW MetroRider MF158/19	MCW	B33F	1988
46	J16043	Leyland Swift LBM6T/2R	Wadham Stringer Vanguard	B43F	1991
47	J14972	Ford R1014	Duple Dominant	B41F	1977
48	J16439	Leyland Swift LBM6T/2R	Wadham Stringer Vanguard	B43F	1991
49	J14951	Ford R1014	Duple Dominant	B41F	1977
50	J71210	MCW MetroRider MF158/19	MCW	B33F	1988

52-64

		Ford R1014	Duple Dominant	B41F	1978-83

52	J58923	55	J58126	58	J16601	61	J31271	63	J31300
53	J58125	56	J58127	59	J16598	62	J31281	64	J31312
54	J58128	57	J16527	60	J16582				

Special Liveries:
Overall Advertisements: Almost all of the fleet is in advertising liveries.